Gluten-Free Christmas Cookies

Ellen Brown

CIDER MILL PRESS

BOOK PUBLISHERS

Kennebunkport, Maine

Cider Mill Press Book Publishers
"Where good books are ready for press"
12 Port Farm Road
Kennebunkport, Maine 04046

Visit us on the Web!
www.cidermillpress.com

Cover design by Whitney Cookman
Interior design by Alicia Freile, Tango Media
Typset by Gwen Galeone
Typography: Chaparral Pro, Helvetica Neue, and Latino Rumba

Printed in China

1 2 3 4 5 6 7 8 9 0
First Edition

Contents

Introduction 5

Chapter 1: Approved Ingredients: The Gluten-Free Pantry 8

Chapter 2: In the Beginning: General Pointers for All Baking..........................16

Chapter 3: Merrily We Roll Along: Cutout and Formed Cookies....................26

Chapter 4: Piles of Perfection: Drop Cookies 52

Chapter 5: Luscious Layers: Bar Cookies and Brownies.................................72

Chapter 6: Gluten-Free from the Start: Meringues and Macaroons 92

Chapter 7: Candy Is Dandy: Unbaked Gluten-Free Confections 106

Index 127

PREFACE

Christmas means "visions of sugarplums" and allowing cautious eating to take a holiday in order to savor each and every sugarplum. But for the millions of people for whom eating gluten, a natural protein found in wheat flour, is tantamount to munching poison, that's hardly the case. They have to be vigilant about every morsel they put in their mouths every day of the year.

There's no magic wand that can be waved over a baked good to make it free from gluten, nor is there any one product that can replace wheat flour on a one-to-one basis. But with just a few ingredients—all of them totally natural— your cookies can be as delicious as any made previously with wheat flour but with one exception: everyone you love can now enjoy them. No one is a second-class citizen who has to be told, "These aren't for you."

And what delicious treats you'll find in this book! All of the basic groups of cookies—from crispy sugar cookies that can be decorated with icing and candies to easy-to-make bar cookies and classic drop cookies—are all included. In addition are some cookie forms, such as meringues and macaroons, which have never contained gluten. These are great cookies to make for gluten-intolerant people if you don't want to buy special flours and starches.

The book ends with a chapter on gluten-free candies. These dense nougat and fudge treats are also part of Christmas celebrations, and they can be made on top of the stove while the oven is filled with trays of cookies.

If you've been baking gluten-free goodies for years, I hope you'll find some new recipes here to tantalize family and friends. But if you're new to the world of recipes calling for rice flour and potato starch instead of all-purpose flour, you'll find some useful guidance on the hows and whys of gluten-free baking to help you convert cherished family favorites to a gluten-free regimen as well as finding new recipes everyone will enjoy.

Christmas is a time of giving, and what could be a better gift to those who must eliminate gluten from their diets than a feast for their eyes and their tummies.

Happy baking!

Ellen Brown
Providence, RI

INTRODUCTION
No Grain, No Pain

Understanding the need to live gluten-free starts with understanding how gluten can cause life-threatening problems if not removed from the diet of those who cannot tolerate it. But the good news is that following a gluten-free diet can mitigate debilitating symptoms and pain in as little as a few months—using food and not a pharmacy.

Our bodies contain a complex and interlocking system to prevent harm. There is a network of organs, glands, and cell types that are lumped under the heading of the immune system that are all dedicated to warding off illness. But sometimes the immune system has been mysteriously programmed incorrectly and attacks healthy cells rather than potentially harmful ones. These maladies are termed *autoimmune diseases*. And though not fully understood, many medical professionals agree that the sources of autoimmune disorders include viruses, which change the information carried inside the cells; sunlight and other forms of radiation; certain chemicals; and drugs. There may also be a link between autoimmune diseases and sex hormones since many more women suffer than do men.

There are more than eighty types of autoimmune disease, and they include lupus, rheumatoid arthritis, and Graves' disease. (Some medical authorities also believe that multiple sclerosis is caused by an autoimmune response.) While the aggravating factors in many of these diseases are complex, in the case of celiac disease it is really rather easy. Celiac disease is caused by an autoimmune response to gluten, one of the thirty proteins found in wheat, barley, and rye.

Humans as a species are unable to properly digest the gluten protein. Normal protein digestion involves a complete breakdown of protein into small particle called amino acids that are in turn absorbed by the small intestine and used by the body as a nutritional source. Those without gluten intolerance don't appear to be affected negatively by the inability to properly digest gluten in the way those with gluten intolerance are.

But for those who are intolerant, the undigested gluten protein gets absorbed into the lining of the small intestine but is not seen by the body as a source of nutrition. To the contrary, the body's immune system attacks these protein particles as something that needs to be destroyed, in very much the same way as it would attack an invading organism such as a virus, bacteria, or parasite. This causes inflammation and damage to the small intestine, which prevents it from absorbing the nutrients your body needs to remain healthy.

Normally, the small intestine is lined with tiny, hair-like projections called *villi* that resemble the deep pile of a plush carpet on a microscopic scale. It is these villi that work to absorb vitamins, minerals, and other nutrients from the food you eat. Without prominent villi, the inner surface of the small intestine becomes less like a plush carpet and more like a tile floor. The body is unable to absorb nutrients necessary for health and growth, so malnutrition results.

It is now clear that the disease is far more common than doctors once believed. New research reveals that celiac disease may be one of the most common genetic diseases, and one federal study estimates that 1 in every

133 Americans suffers from it. That's more than 3 million people.

The condition is diagnosed by testing for three antibodies—*anti-gliadin*, *anti-endomysial*, and *anti-tissue transglutaminase*—all of which are present when an affected person is exposed to gluten, but disappear when the offending grains are no longer consumed.

But there are millions more people whose digestive problems don't fall under the strict definition of celiac disease (because they do not test positively for the antibodies), but who have found that following a gluten-free diet helps them. Rather than calling them gluten-intolerant, they're termed gluten-sensitive, and this group could include up to thirty percent of the American population.

For this much larger group, removing gluten can eliminate symptoms ranging from abdominal pain to osteoporosis and sinus congestion. Gluten-sensitivity has also been linked to conditions such as psoriasis, anemia, and asthma.

Following a gluten-free diet is not a temporary measure to ameliorate a condition. It's for life. Eliminating gluten doesn't cause the body to become less sensitive to it. The condition will return as soon as gluten is reintroduced to the diet.

But these days, following a gluten-free diet is easier than ever before. According to a study released in 2009, the market for gluten-free products grew at a compound annual growth rate of 28 percent from 2004 to 2008, capturing almost $1.6 billion in retail sales during 2008. It's anticipated that by 2012 the market will reach $2.6 billion in sales.

This increase in gluten-free foods makes it possible to find the ingredients needed for the delicious cookies in this book in general supermarkets rather than health food specialty shops. The recipes were formulated so that everyone will love them, and for those on a gluten-free diet it means they can enjoy sweet treats again.

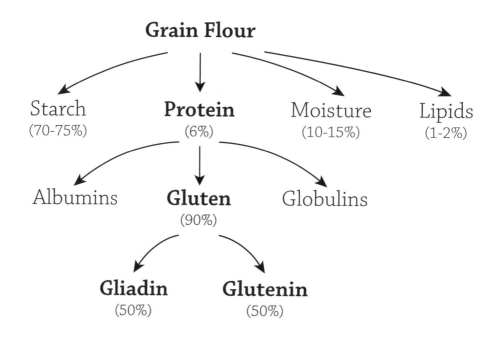

Grain Flour

Starch (70-75%) **Protein** (6%) Moisture (10-15%) Lipids (1-2%)

Albumins **Gluten** (90%) Globulins

Gliadin (50%) **Glutenin** (50%)

CHAPTER 1:

Approved Ingredients:
The Gluten-Free Pantry

Many of the ingredients used to make the cookies in this book are very familiar. They've been part of every cook's repertoire since that first venture into the kitchen to make a batch of brownies as a child. Our old friends eggs, butter, baking soda, and vanilla make many appearances throughout the book.

The dough or batter can be flavored with chocolate in many forms, as well as by adding citrus and other fruits. Some recipes contain crunchy nuts, while others have succulent dried fruits folded in. And the forms of cookies are familiar too; dough is rolled and cut into fun shapes, dropped onto baking sheets, or baked in a large pan and cut after cooking.

But one ingredient crucial to traditional baking is not listed—all-purpose flour. And that omission creates a sea change. There is no one powdery substance that can take the place of wheat flour and the gluten produced by two of its inherent proteins.

Gluten is a beautiful thing. Who doesn't love a crispy gingerbread person or a chewy chocolate chip cookie? Gluten has traditionally been the way to achieve this range of textures.

In order to make gluten-free cookies just as tantalizing as ones made with wheat flour requires more than one dry ingredient, and a slightly different proportion of dry and wet components. In this chapter you will learn about these all-natural foods, and the role they play in creating cookies that will bring a sparkle to everyone's eyes.

The Role of Gluten in Traditional Baking

While there's some science involved with all cooking, when the end result is a baked good, science and art are given almost equal billing. While eliminating rye and barley from the diet presents some challenges, eliminating all forms of wheat and wheat flour is a Herculean task—especially when baking. For centuries, wheat flour has been the key ingredient in which all recipes have been developed.

Wheat flour contains as many as thirty proteins, and two of those—glutenin and gliadin—form gluten when stirred with moisture. These two proteins grab water and connect to form elastic strands of gluten. If flour has a lot of these proteins, it grabs up water faster, making the strong and springy gluten that is needed to bake bread. If there are fewer proteins, or if the proteins are coated with fat to become shorter, the gluten creates tenderness as in piecrust.

The formation of this elastic gluten network serves many functions in a recipe. Like a net, gluten traps and holds air bubbles. They later expand from the gas created by a leavening agent such as baking soda or baking powder. When a recipe is baked, the stretched flour proteins become rigid as moisture evaporates from the heat of the oven and sets the baked goods' structure.

Replicating this structure is no easy task. There is no way to remove the gluten from wheat flour because the proteins are built into the DNA of the wheat plant. But by adding a few other dry powders, the results can be just as good.

Reading Ingredient Labels

When you're looking for wheat on those ingredient labels, beware! Wheat is often disguised and there are other ways it can be listed. Both kamut and faro are ancient types of wheat, and bulgur is cracked wheat kernels. Also be on the lookout for couscous, which, contrary to popular belief, is not a grain but a granular pasta made with wheat flour. Other ways wheat flour is listed include semolina, farina, and durum. If you see a product with one of these names, it contains gluten.

Gluten-Free Flours and Starches

Here's the bad news: there is no one ingredient with which you can make a one-to-one substitution for all-purpose wheat flour when making gluten-free baked goods. But here's the good news: while the recipes might appear long because you need several ingredients to create the same texture you'd get if you could use wheat flour, the ingredients are readily available even in general supermarkets.

If you visit the gluten-free baking aisle of supermarkets or search online, you'll discover a dizzying array of products that can be used to replace wheat flour. And in addition to being free of gluten, many of them are far more nutritious than wheat flour.

Each substance in the gluten-free arsenal has different properties. One will strengthen, another will act as a tenderizer, and yet another will add moisture. Wheat has all of these properties, which is why it is difficult to understand needing multiple flours to substitute for just one.

There are two basic categories of ingredients:

• **Protein/fiber flours**, such as white and brown rice flour, provide structure, stability, color, texture, and nutrition. Some flours in this category, such as bean flour and chestnut flour, add flavor as well as texture, so they are not used very often, if at all, for cookies. But they should be used for breads and other gluten-free general cooking.

• **Starches**, such as cornstarch, tapioca starch, potato starch, and sweet rice flour, are very fine in texture and create baked goods that have a soft crumb and a smooth texture.

Protein/fiber flours are heavy and baked goods made with them end up very dense. Starches alone cannot provide enough structure for baked goods to hold their shape. Successful gluten-free baking begins with using the right flour blend with *both* protein/fiber flours and starches together to get good results. The right combination can produce excellent results, often indistinguishable from baked goods made with wheat.

Flours should be stored refrigerated after opening, while starches can be stored at room temperature. If you have pre-mixed a baking mix, it's best to store it refrigerated if you have space.

Note that the ingredients listed below are used for cookies; if this was a book on gluten-free breads or general gluten-free cooking, the list would be far longer and include flour made from such grains as millet and garbanzo beans.

Almond Meal: Of the nut flours, this is the only one that is available pre-packaged because it has been used for centuries for many desserts, such as classic French *macarons*. You can grind blanched almonds in a coffee grinder or mini-food processor to make your own. You can also substitute such nuts as peeled hazelnuts.

Amaranth Flour: Amaranth is a tiny seed native to Central America; it was one of the primary grains raised by the Aztecs. The flour is much higher in lysine, an essential amino acid, than other grain flours. When amaranth is combined with cornmeal it creates a complete protein like that found in meat or poultry.

Arrowroot: This starchy flour, made by drying and grinding the roots of a tropical tuber, has twice the thickening power of wheat flour and is completely tasteless. It is most often used to thicken sauces and puddings but can also be used in baked goods. It can be substituted on a one-to-one basis for cornstarch.

Cornmeal: We are all familiar with cornmeal, and it is important to buy it from a manufacturer who processes it in a facility not contaminated with gluten. Cornmeal is made by grinding dried corn kernels, and it can be fine-, medium-, or coarse-textured. Water-ground or stone-ground types are more nutritious than steel-ground, since more of the corn kernel is retained.

Cornstarch: Along with arrowroot, cornstarch is what is most often used to thicken gluten-free foods. Called corn flour in some countries, it should never be confused

Sweet Rice Flour: Called *mochiko* in Japanese, it can be found in Asian markets as well as supermarkets, and while called sweet there is no sweetening added. It's made from glutinous short-grained Japanese rice, and it makes cookie dough pliable and somewhat sticky. If you are out of sweet rice flour, the closest substitution is tapioca starch.

Tapioca Starch: Also called "cassava flour," it's derived from the yucca plant, which is a starchy tropical tuber. It adds body to cookies as well as a chewy texture, and it helps baked goods to brown.

What About Oats?

Including oats as part of a gluten-free diet has been controversial, but recent research has spurred many organizations to give oats the thumbs up. While oats *do not contain gluten*, the problem is possible contamination of oats with gluten-containing grains grown nearby. Pure oats—those not contaminated by other grains—are recommended by a majority of celiac organizations in North America, and the packaging should say gluten-free or non-contaminated.

with cornmeal. Cornstarch is made by grinding the endosperm of the corn kernel after the kernels have been steeped for a few days, which makes it possible to separate the germ from the endosperm.

Potato Starch: Potato starch is very different from potato flour, so be careful when you shop for it. Potato starch is made from raw potatoes, while potato flour is made from cooked potatoes. The flour is far denser, and the two cannot be substituted for each other.

Rice Flour: This neutral-flavored flour is one of the most common substitutes for all-purpose wheat flour. Both white and brown rice can be made into flour, but the outer husk is always removed before grinding. Brown rice flour has a better nutritional profile because it does contain some fiber. I use both for these cookie recipes, and the choice really depends on the desired color of the baked cookie.

Gums As Binders

Gluten gives cookie doughs and batters strength, so that the air incorporated by yeast or chemical leavening agents is trapped until the heat of the oven cooks the proteins and forms a structure. Your gluten-free cookies might end up as a pile of crumbs without the addition of natural gums to serve as binders and give gluten-free flours and starches that all-important "stretch factor." They also give doughs and batters an inherent stickiness.

The two different powdered products that can be used interchangeably are *xanthan* (pronounced *ZAHN-thun*) gum and *guar* (pronounced *gwar*) gum. They are mixed with the dry ingredients.

Xanthan gum is sometimes called *corn sugar gum*. It's a natural carbohydrate that isn't absorbed by the body. The additive is produced by the fermentation of the bacteria *Xanthomonas campestris*. When this bacteria is combined with corn sugar it creates a colorless slime, which is then dehydrated and ground into xanthan gum.

The guar plant, also known as a *cluster plant*, grows primarily in areas of Pakistan and the northern parts of India that share a climate of alternating monsoons and droughts. Guar is an important crop in these regions. The plants are harvested after the monsoon season and the seeds are allowed to dry in the sun. The seeds are then manually or mechanically separated and processed into powder or sold as split seeds.

> You've eaten xanthan gum many times, and if you see it on a label, relax! It's a real food and not something out of a test tube. Manufacturers add xanthan gum to candy to prevent sugar crystals from forming and to many ice creams to give them a smooth texture and mouth feel.

Basic Baking Mixture and Recipe Conversion

The correct percentage of flour and starch to use depends on the type of baked good you're making. When baking with wheat flour there is a wide range available depending on the use. For example, bread flour is very high in protein from its base of hard wheat, and cake flour is very low in protein and is comprised of soft wheat; all-purpose flour blends the two.

While there are a few all-purpose gluten-free baking blends on the market, I think designing a specific mix for the type of baked good is preferable. This formulation is one I devised that works for many cookie recipes—from crispy to chewy and light to dense— and it can be used blended in a one-to-one substitution for all-purpose wheat flour. Use this formulation when converting family favorites for gluten-free baking, but when using one of the recipes in this book, use the precise formulation given with each recipe.

My Basic Baking Mix is based on rice flour with a few starches plus xanthan gum. You can substitute up to 1 cup of almond meal for 1 cup of the rice flour for nut cookies.

Basic Baking Mix

Makes 3 cups

Ingredients
2 cups white or brown rice flour
⅓ cup sweet rice flour
⅓ cup potato starch
⅓ cup tapioca starch
2 teaspoons xanthan gum

Mix all ingredients together, and store refrigerated in an airtight container.

Other Helpful Ingredients

While gluten-free baking presents some unique challenges, other than the choice of dry ingredients, the recipes in this book utilize the classics.

Eggs: Without the protein being supplied by the gluten in the flour, eggs take on a more important role; they are another great source of protein and can create the structure of baked goods. In addition to providing protein, they also create the steam needed for starches to become firm. Egg yolk is also a rich source of emulsifying agents that makes it easier to incorporate air into the doughs and batters due to its fat and lecithin content.

Sugar: Sugar adds sweetness, as well as contributing to the browning process that takes place when a baked good is cooked. The browning occurs when the sugar reacts with the protein in eggs and the dairy solids of butter during baking, and the higher the sugar content of cookie dough, the browner it will become once baked. Sugar also holds moisture, which extends the life of cookies. Along with solid fat, it is the crystals of sugar that make small holes that are expanded by leavening agents.

> **The granulated sugar we take for granted today as a staple was once so rare and expensive it was called "white gold." Sugar cane, the first source of sugar, is a perennial grass that originated in Asia, but is now grown in virtually every tropical and subtropical region of the world. It was only during the nineteenth century that refining beets for their sugar became commonplace.**

Fats: In all baking where solid fats are creamed with crystalline sugar, tiny air cells are incorporated into the batter, so the baked good will have a fine, aerated texture. Fat is also responsible for providing lubrication and a luxurious mouth feel. I am a devotee of only baking with unsalted butter. The milk fat in butter contributes tenderness, color, and helps build the structure of the baked good. But most importantly, it releases its delicious flavor.

Leavening Agents: A leavening agent is anything that creates volume in baked goods by foaming. Air is a natural leavener, which is why so many cookie doughs specify to beat the butter and sugar until that wonderful state of "light and fluffy." The lightness and the fluffiness is the air that's incorporated.

But most of the time, the leavening is left to two primary chemical agents: baking soda and baking powder. Both of these produce carbon dioxide when they are mixed with moisture. Baking soda, also called bicarbonate of soda, must be combined with an acidic ingredient like buttermilk to create carbon dioxide, while baking powder is a combination of baking soda and cream of tartar, which is acidic. Baking soda is twice as strong as baking powder, but the two can be substituted for one another.

It is important to look at baking powder carefully, however. Some brands use a small percentage of wheat starch as the "moisture absorption agent." Most, however, use cornstarch or potato starch, including such leading brands as Rumford and Davis. But do check labels carefully.

> **Chemical leavening is nothing new. Amelia Simmons used pearl ash in her book, *American Cookery*, published in 1796. Because carbon dioxide is released at a faster rate through the acid-base reaction than through the fermentation process provided by living yeast, breads made with chemical leavening became known as "quick breads" more than a century ago.**

Avoiding Contamination

If you're new to gluten-free baking, or you're making these cookies and other treats as a gift for someone who must follow a gluten-free diet, the whole concept of contamination is perhaps new to you. Setting up a system so that foods containing gluten and gluten-free foods never meet can take time, but it is time well spent. Here are some rules to follow to ensure that your gluten-free products are not inadvertently contaminated by wheat flour or any gluten-containing food:

- Thoroughly wash out cabinets where gluten-free products will be stored and make sure everyone who uses the kitchen is aware that these cabinets contain only gluten-free food. However, unless the kitchen is to be free of all gluten-containing foods, it's still wise to place gluten-free ingredients in airtight containers before storing them.
- Clean all the kitchen surfaces thoroughly before starting to prepare gluten-free dishes, and then change the dishrag and dishtowel for a fresh one. Don't use a sponge because it cannot be properly cleaned to make it free from gluten. The same is true for porous surfaces such as wooden cutting boards. Have special ones for gluten-free ingredients.
- Have separate containers of butter or margarine for gluten-free baking. Crumbs from someone's morning toast could have landed on a stick of butter at breakfast.
- Don't use the same sifter for gluten-free and regular flours. Clearly label the gluten-free sifter to avoid mistakes.
- Have separate containers of ingredients for all gluten-free baking. Even though there is no gluten in granulated sugar or baking soda, molecules of wheat flour could have landed on them.
- Always place the gluten-free foods on the top shelf of the oven to avoid the risk of spills onto it. The same is true in the refrigerator; the gluten-free foods should be on higher shelves.
- Foil is a great way to avoid contamination. Use foil to keep foods separate when preparing, cooking, or storing.
- Use stickers of different colors when storing gluten-free foods to segregate them from other foods.

CHAPTER 2:

In the Beginning:
General Pointers for All Baking

B aking cookies is not rocket science, which is perhaps why it's the first kitchen activity most of us undertook as children. In this chapter, there are some pointers to ensure that you're a "smart cookie" every time you bake. These are general tips to help you with all your baking and cooking, not just gluten-free cookies.

Baking Basics

Even though cooking is an art form, when it comes to baking, science class enters the equation as well. While savory recipes are tolerant of virtually endless substitutions, baked goods are not. Each ingredient performs a specific function in a recipe based on a certain quantity to create a batter or dough. These are some general pointers on procedures to be used for all genres of baked goods:

• **Measure accurately.** Measure dry ingredients in dry measuring cups, which are plastic or metal, and come in sizes of ¼, ⅓, ½, ¾, and 1 cup. Spoon dry ingredients from the container or canister into the measuring cup, and then sweep the top with a straight edge such as the back of a knife or a spatula to measure it properly. Do not dip the cup into the canister or tap it on the counter to produce a level surface. These methods pack down the dry ingredients and can increase the actual volume by up to 10 percent. Tablespoons and teaspoons should also be leveled; a rounded ½ teaspoon can really measure almost 1 teaspoon. If the box or can does not have a straight edge built in, level the excess in the spoon back into the container with the back of a knife blade. Measure liquids in liquid measures, which come in different sizes, but are transparent glass or plastic and have lines on the sides. To accurately measure liquids, place the measuring cup on a flat counter, and bend down to read the marked level at eye level.

• **Create a consistent temperature.** All ingredients should be at room temperature unless otherwise indicated. Having all ingredients at the same temperature makes it easier to combine them into a smooth, homogeneous mixture. Adding cold liquid to a dough or batter can cause the batter to lose its unified structure by making the fat rigid.

• **Preheat the oven.** Some ovens can take up to 25 minutes to reach a high temperature, such as 450°F. The minimum heating time should be 15 minutes.

• **Plan ahead.** Read the recipe thoroughly, and assemble all your ingredients. This means that you have accounted for all ingredients required for a recipe in advance, so you don't get to a step and realize you must improvise. Assembling in advance also lessens the risk of over-mixing dough or batters, as the mixer drones on while you search for a specific spice or bag of chips.

Careful Creaming

Perhaps the most vital step in the creation of a cookie dough is the "creaming" of the butter and sugar. During this process, air is beaten in and trapped in the butter's crystalline structure. It is the number and size of the air bubbles (which then become enlarged by the carbon dioxide produced by baking soda or baking powder) that leavens a dough or batter to produce a high, finely-textured product.

The starting point in proper creaming is to ensure that the butter is at the correct temperature, approximately 70°F. Remove butter from the refrigerator and cut each stick into approximately 30 slices. Allow them to sit at room temperature for 15 to 20 minutes to soften.

Begin creaming by beating the butter alone in a mixer until it has broken into small pieces. Then add

Chocolate 101

The key to the success for all chocolate desserts is to use a high-quality product. It's also important (with the following exceptions) to use the type of chocolate specified in the recipe, because the amount of additional sugar and other ingredients are calculated according to the sweetness level of the chocolate. If you use a different chocolate, things could taste off. Now on to the sweet stuff. Here's a quick guide to chocolate:

• **Unsweetened.** Also referred to as baking or bitter chocolate, this is the purest of all cooking chocolate. It is hardened chocolate liquor (the essence of the cocoa bean, not an alcohol) that contains no sugar. It is usually packaged in a bar of 8 (1-ounce) blocks. According to the U.S. standard of identity, unsweetened chocolate must contain 50 to 58 percent cocoa butter.

• **Bittersweet.** This chocolate is slightly sweetened with sugar, and the amount varies depending on the manufacturer. This chocolate must contain 35 percent chocolate liquor and should be used when intense chocolate flavor is desired. Also use it interchangeably with semisweet chocolate in cooking and baking.

the sugar and beat at medium speed to start the process of combining them. Then increase the speed to high and scrape the bowl frequently. When properly creamed, the texture of the butter and sugar mixture will be light and fluffy.

- **Semisweet.** This chocolate is sweetened with sugar, but unlike bittersweet, it also can have added flavorings such as vanilla. It is available in bar form as well as chips and pieces.
- **Sweet cooking.** This chocolate must contain 15 percent chocolate liquor, and it almost always has a higher sugar content than semisweet chocolate. It is usually found in 4-ounce bars.
- **Milk.** This is a mild-flavored chocolate used primarily for candy bars but rarely (except for milk chocolate chips) in baking. It can have as little as 10 percent chocolate liquor but must contain 12 percent milk solids.
- **Unsweetened cocoa powder.** This is powdered chocolate that has had a portion of the cocoa butter removed. Cocoa keeps indefinitely in a cool place.
- **Dutch process cocoa powder.** This type of cocoa powder is formulated with reduced acidity and gives foods a mellower flavor. However, it also burns at a lower temperature than more common cocoa.

> **Like fine wine, dark chocolate actually improves with age. Store it tightly wrapped in a cool place. Even if the chocolate has developed a gray "bloom" from being stored at too high a temperature, it is still fine to use for cooking.**

Subbing With Success

Bittersweet, semisweet, and sweet chocolate can be used interchangeably in recipes, depending on personal taste. Most chocolate desserts tend to be sweet, so it's better to go from a semisweet to a bittersweet rather than the other direction.

Do not substitute chocolate chips and bits of broken chocolate for one another. Chocolate chips are formulated to retain their shape at high heat and react differently when baked than chopped chocolate does. Chocolate chips can form gritty granules in a cooled dessert.

Handle with Care

Except when you're eating chocolate out of your hand or folding chips into cookie dough, chocolate needs a bit of special handling. Use these tips when dealing with the common tasks associated with chocolate:

Chopping chocolate. Chopping it into fine pieces makes melting easier. You can do this in a food processor fitted with a steel blade. Begin by breaking it with a heavy knife rather than breaking it with your hands. Body heat is sufficiently high enough to soften the chocolate so it will not chop evenly.

Melting chocolate. Most chocolate needs careful melting because it scorches easily. You can melt it in a number of ways:

1. Melt chunks in the top of a double boiler placed over barely simmering water.

2. Melt chopped chocolate in a microwave-safe bowl, and microwave on Medium (50 percent power) for 30 seconds. Stir, and repeat as necessary.

3. Preheat the oven to 250°F. Place the chopped chocolate in the oven and then turn off the heat immediately. Stir after 3 minutes, and return to the warm oven if necessary.

With all these methods, melt the chocolate until it is just about smooth; the heat in the chocolate will complete the process.

> **An easy way to dress up bar cookies is by drizzling the pan with dark chocolate or white chocolate before cutting the cookies into pieces. Once the chocolate is melted, dip a spoon into it and then wave the spoon over the cookie pan. An alternate method is to place the melted chocolate in a heavy re-sealable plastic bag, and cut off the tip of one corner.**

Important Equipment

There is very little specialized equipment needed for baking cookies regardless if they are gluten-free or not. Here is a list of the machines and gadgets I used on a regular basis while developing the recipes for this book:

• **Candy/deep fry thermometer.** While in Chapter 7, I give the time-honored visual and textural clues for determining the temperature of sugar syrup, which is vital to all candies and some cookies too, being able to take an accurate reading takes all the anxiety out of these recipes.

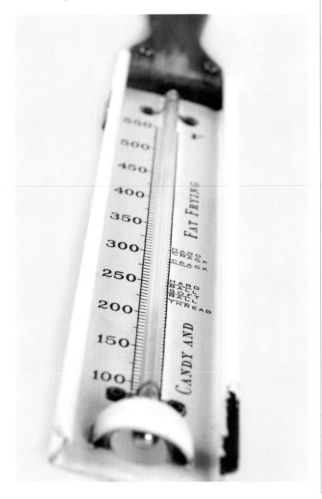

• **Microplane grater.** This resembles a flat kitchen spatula but with tiny holes in it. It's fabulous for grating citrus zest and fibrous foods such as ginger, and you can also use it for Parmesan cheese and even garlic cloves for other recipes.

• **Food processor.** There is a dedicated corner of my dishwasher given over to the workhorse of the kitchen. While the base needs to be cleaned thoroughly before making any gluten-free item, for very little money you can purchase a second work bowl. The work bowl of food processors is made of plastic, which can harbor food particles once scratched.

• **Wire cooling racks.** These are essential and there's really no substitute. The type of rack on top of a broiler pan is too solid, and there's nothing that makes crispy cookies soggy faster than placing them on an impervious surface.

• **A powerful mixer.** Some of these cookie doughs are very thick, and a standard mixer that sits on the counter is the best friend you can have. While hand-held mixers are fine for small tasks, the stand mixer is what is best for baking. The balloon whip attachment is wonderful for meringues, and the paddle makes the thickest substance look easy to blend.

• **Offset spatulas.** These are the type of spatula with the handle raised up from the level of the blade so that transferring cookies from the baking sheets to the cooling racks is comfortable and easy.

Devising a Cookie "Game Plan"

Around the holidays, kitchen efficiency becomes even more important because there's so much cooking to do, in addition to all the other activities that surround the approach of Christmas. If you have a few hours to spend in the kitchen, you want to make sure your cookie production is high.

Start by making a pan of bar cookies; they are quick to assemble but they take the longest time to bake. Once they are in the oven, it's time to make the doughs for rolled cookies that need chilling before they can be baked.

The third type of cookie to make is a batch of drop cookies. The bars are out of the oven, and these cookies don't need chilling time, so they can bake while you roll and cut out the chilled doughs.

Almost all cookies in this book are baked at 350°F, so there's no need for the oven to ever be empty. If you choose a recipe that is baked at 375°F, make those after the other batches.

And last, but hardly least, are meringues. They are left in a cool oven for many hours, so they come at the end of the baking cycle. But remember that they're in the oven before you start to bake again! I've ruined many a batch by preheating the oven the next day to a high temperature, forgetting they were still inside.

Becoming a Pastry Picasso

Cookies painted with icing or decorated with candies are almost the definition of Christmas cookies, and you'll find many recipes for them in Chapter 3. In this section, you'll learn ways to decorate them both before and after baking.

Confectioners' Sugar Glaze

This is the easiest and most basic way to cover cooled cookies, and it hardens in less than an hour.

Yield: 1½ cups
Active time: 5 minutes
Start to finish: 5 minutes

Ingredients
4 cups (1 pound) confectioners' sugar
4 to 5 tablespoons water
½ teaspoon clear vanilla extract
Food coloring (optional)

1. Combine confectioners' sugar, 4 tablespoons water, and vanilla in a mixing bowl. Stir until smooth, adding additional water if too thick.

2. If tinting the glaze, transfer it to small cups and add food coloring, a few drops at a time, until desired color is reached. Stir well before adding additional coloring.

Note: The glaze can be kept at room temperature in an airtight container, with a sheet of plastic wrap pressed directly into the surface, for up 6 hours. Beat it again lightly to emulsify before using.

Variations
✳ *Substitute orange juice for the water and orange extract for the vanilla.*
✳ *Substitute peppermint oil or almond extract for the vanilla.*

How to Use
This glaze is not strong enough to hold large candies, but it can be used as "glue" for small items like jimmies. One way to use it is to spread the white glaze on cooled cookies and allow it to dry hard. Then mix 1 teaspoon of water into ¼ cup of the glaze, and tint it with food coloring. Crumple up a sheet of waxed paper and dip it into the tinted glaze; then dab the cookies and you'll have a marbled effect.

Royal Icing

This is the formulation for the shiny icing used on cookies once they're baked and cooled. This frosting can only be used on cookies kept at room temperature because refrigerating the cookies can cause the frosting to become sticky.

Yield: 3½ cups
Active time: 5 minutes
Start to finish: 12 minutes

Ingredients
3 large egg whites, at room temperature
½ teaspoon cream of tartar
¼ teaspoon salt
4 cups (1 pound) confectioners' sugar
½ teaspoon pure vanilla extract
Food coloring (optional)

1. Place egg whites in a grease-free mixing bowl and beat at medium speed with an electric mixer until frothy. Add the cream of tartar and salt, raise the speed to high, and beat until soft peaks form.

2. Add sugar and beat at low speed to moisten. Raise the speed to high, and beat for 5 to 7 minutes, or until mixture is glossy and stiff peaks form. Beat in vanilla.

3. If tinting icing, transfer it to small cups and add food coloring, a few drops at a time, until desired consistency is reached. Stir well before adding additional coloring.

Note: The icing can be kept at room temperature in an airtight container for up to 2 days. Beat it again lightly to emulsify before using.

Variations
✳ *Substitute peppermint oil, almond extract, lemon oil, or orange oil for the vanilla.*

How to Use
Royal Icing of this consistency is perfect to pipe decorations onto cooled cookies, and you can also use it as the "glue" to affix candies. If you want to paint the cookies with frosting, thin the icing with milk in 1-teaspoon amounts until the proper consistency is reached.

Buttercream Icing

This icing is richer than Royal Icing, and it is also not bright white because it's made with butter. It does harden somewhat, but not into a true glaze.

Yield: 2½ cups
Active time: 5 minutes
Start to finish: 5 minutes

Ingredients
¼ pound (1 stick) unsalted butter, softened
4 cups (1 pound) confectioners' sugar
3 tablespoons milk
1 teaspoon pure vanilla extract
Food coloring (optional)

1. Place butter, sugar, milk, and vanilla in a large mixing bowl. Beat at low speed with an electric mixer to combine. Increase the speed to high, and beat for 2 minutes, or until light and fluffy.

2. If tinting icing, transfer it to small cups and add food coloring, a few drops at a time, until desired color is reached. Stir well before adding additional coloring.

Note: The icing can be kept refrigerated in an airtight container for up to 5 days. Bring it to room temperature before using.

Variations
* *Substitute almond extract, lemon oil, or orange oil for the vanilla.*

How to Use
Buttercream is a wonderful icing to use to make rosettes or other complex decorations with a pastry bag. Add additional confectioners' sugar in 1-tablespoon increments if not stiff enough.

Egg Paint

Mixing beaten egg yolks with food coloring produces far more vibrant colors than can be created with Royal Icing. It's like the tempera paint used in Medieval European churches.

Ingredients
4-5 egg yolks
Food coloring

1. Whisk about 4 or 5 egg yolks well, and divide them into different small cups.

2. Add food coloring at about the ratio of ½ teaspoon per egg yolk, and stir well.

3. Start by drawing a design on the cookies with the tip of a paring knife; the grooves will keep the colors from running into each other.

4. Use a small paintbrush to apply the color to cookies before they are baked. The colors will darken slightly in the oven.

Note: Pastry brushes are expensive, but paintbrushes are cheap. Any natural-bristle paintbrush can be used as a pastry brush.

Using Candies and Confections

The collection of colored and flavored sweets that can be affixed to cookies is almost endless. Some of them should be applied before the cookies are baked, and others need to be "glued" on with Royal Icing once cooled.

As a general rule, any candy that can melt, like hard candies, miniature marshmallows, or jellybeans, should be applied after cooking, and any candy that is basically an ingredient, such as the coarse colored sugars found around the holidays, gold or silver dragées, nuts, or candied fruit, should be used before baking. Ingredients such as raisins can be used either way. If they are the "eyes" of gingerbread people or snowmen, it's probably best to place them before baking, but if they're ornaments on a wreath, it's best to add them after the cookie has been frosted.

A way to use colored sugars after cookies are baked is to create patterns with stencils. Spread either Royal Icing or Confectioners' Sugar Glaze on the cooled cookie, and then place a stencil made from parchment paper over it. Sprinkle sugars or jimmies through the hole in the stencil.

CHAPTER 3:

Merrily We Roll Along:
Cutout and Formed Cookies

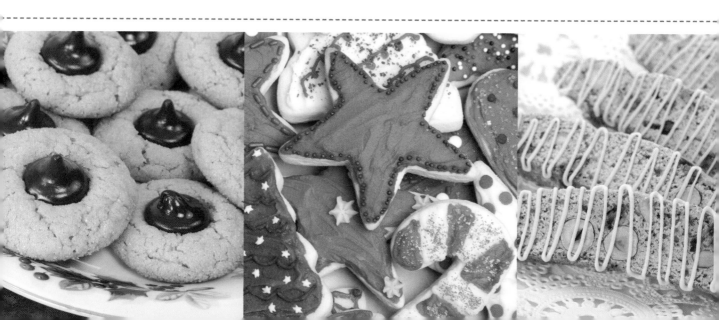

"Christmas cookie" is almost synonymous with a crispy, buttery cookie in a fanciful shape, decorated with colored icing and perhaps some candies, too. And right behind that image are gingerbread people with tiny smiling faces and buttons down their "jackets." You'll be happy to know that these perennial favorites are easily made using gluten-free ingredients.

Because there's no gluten to create dough stiff enough to roll, compensations must be made. You'll find that time is needed to chill the dough well. This allows for the butter, which was softened during the mixing process, to become firm once again. After that occurs, rolling these cookies thin enough to cut out is very easy.

Once the dough is rolled and you've used a cutter to create your shape, it's easier to remove the excess dough rather than trying to move the delicate cookies to the baking sheets. This process is similar to what artists term relief sculpture. What you are doing is pulling out what is not needed to leave what you want. If you rolled and cut the cookies on a sheet of waxed paper, all you have to do is invert it onto the cookie sheet.

In addition to cookies made with rolled dough, this chapter also contains other traditional forms, such as thumbprints and biscotti. While no piece of equipment similar to a rolling pin is necessary to make them, they are formed by hand to give them a uniform look.

Note: Unless otherwise noted, use these directions for storing cookies in this chapter: keep cookies in an airtight container, layered between sheets of waxed paper or parchment, at room temperature for up to 5 days. Cookies can also be frozen for up to two months. Do not freeze cookies if decorated.

Christmas Sugar Cookies

These cookies are to Christmas what a blank canvas is to an artist. From here the possibilities are endless. Sugar cookies have a delicious buttery flavor and come out of the oven very crisp as well.

Yield: 2 to 4 dozen, depending on the size of the cutters used

Active time: 30 minutes

Start to finish: 1¾ hours, including 1 hour to chill dough

1½ cups amaranth flour

1 cup confectioners' sugar

½ cup cornstarch

1 teaspoon xanthan gum

1 teaspoon cream of tartar

Pinch of salt

½ pound (2 sticks) unsalted butter, cut into thin slices

1 large egg

1 tablespoon whole milk

1 teaspoon pure vanilla extract

Sweet rice flour

Royal Icing (page 23) (optional)

Buttercream Icing (page 24) (optional)

Gluten-free candy decorations (optional)

1. Combine amaranth flour, confectioners' sugar, cornstarch, xanthan gum, cream of tartar, and salt in a food processor fitted with a steel blade. Blend for 5 seconds. Add butter to the work bowl, and process, using on-and-off pulsing, until mixture resembles coarse meal.

2. Combine egg, milk, and vanilla in a small cup, and whisk well. Drizzle liquid into the work bowl, and pulse about 10 times, or until stiff dough forms. If dough is dry and doesn't come together, add additional milk by 1-teaspoon amounts, until dough forms a ball.

3. Divide dough in half and wrap each half in plastic wrap. Press dough into a pancake. Refrigerate dough for 1 hour or until firm (or up to 2 days).

4. Preheat the oven to 350°F. Line two baking sheets with parchment paper or silicon baking mats.

5. Lightly dust a sheet of waxed paper and a rolling pin with sweet rice flour. Roll dough to a thickness of ¼ inch. Dip cookie cutters in sweet rice flour, and cut out cookies. Remove excess dough, and transfer cookies to the baking sheets. Re-roll excess dough, chilling it for 15 minutes if necessary.

6. Bake cookies for 10 to 12 minutes, or until edges are brown. Cool cookies for 2 minutes on the baking sheets, and then transfer them with a spatula to cooling racks to cool completely. Decorate cooled cookies with royal icing and candies, if desired.

Variations
✳ *Substitute lemon oil for the vanilla extract and add 2 teaspoon grated lemon zest to the dough.*
✳ *Substitute ½ cup almond meal for ½ cup of the amaranth flour and substitute almond extract for the vanilla extract.*

> **Gluten-free dough softens faster than dough made with wheat flour, which can make it difficult to handle. One way to mitigate this problem is to place the sheets of rolled out dough in the freezer for 10 to 15 minutes; the dough will then be stiffer.**

Gingerbread People

Redolent with aromatic spices, these traditional cookies can be either painted before baking or decorated after baking.

Yield: 2 to 3 dozen, depending on the size of the cutters used

Active time: 30 minutes

Start to finish: 1¾ hours, including 1 hour to chill dough

1 cup brown rice flour

1 cup cornstarch

2 teaspoons ground ginger

½ teaspoon freshly grated nutmeg

½ teaspoon ground cinnamon

½ teaspoon xanthan gum

½ teaspoon baking soda

¼ teaspoon salt

6 tablespoons (¾ stick) unsalted butter, softened

⅓ cup confectioners' sugar

½ cup dark molasses

½ teaspoon pure vanilla extract

Sweet rice flour

Royal Icing (page 23)

Gluten-free candies (optional)

1. Combine rice flour, cornstarch, ginger, nutmeg, cinnamon, xanthan gum, baking soda, and salt in a mixing bowl. Whisk well.

2. Combine butter and confectioners' sugar in another mixing bowl and beat at low speed with an electric mixer to combine. Increase the speed to high, and beat for 3 to 4 minutes, or until light and fluffy. Add molasses and vanilla, and beat for 1 minute.

3. Slowly add dry ingredients to the butter mixture, and beat until stiff dough forms. Divide dough in half, and wrap each half in plastic wrap. Press dough into a pancake. Refrigerate for 1 hour or until firm, or up to 2 days.

4. Preheat the oven to 350°F. Line two baking sheets with parchment paper or silicon baking mats.

5. Lightly dust a sheet of waxed paper and a rolling pin with sweet rice flour. Roll dough to a thickness of ¼ inch. Dip cookie cutters in sweet rice flour, and cut out cookies. Remove excess dough, and transfer cookies to the baking sheets. Re-roll excess dough, chilling it for 15 minutes if necessary.

6. Bake cookies for 10 to 12 minutes, or until firm. Cool cookies for 2 minutes on the baking sheets, and then transfer them with a spatula to cooling racks to cool completely. Decorate cooled cookies with royal icing and candies.

Variation
✳ *Add ½ cup chopped raisins to the dough, and bake the cookies as drop cookies for 13 to 15 minutes. No chilling is necessary for a drop cookie.*

Spritz

Spritz are drawn from Scandinavian baking. They are the cookies that are pushed through a press into fanciful shapes. This version is flavored with almond and includes almond meal in the dough.

Yield: 3 to 4 dozen

Active time: 20 minutes

Start to finish: 1½ hours, including 1 hour to chill dough

1 cup white rice flour

1 cup confectioners' sugar

½ cup sweet rice flour

½ cup potato starch

½ cup almond meal

1 teaspoon xanthan gum

¼ teaspoon salt

½ pound (2 sticks) unsalted butter, sliced

1 large egg

1 large egg white

1 teaspoon pure vanilla extract

½ teaspoon pure almond extract

Gluten-free sugar sprinkles

Small gluten-free candies

Candied cherries

1. Combine white rice flour, confectioners' sugar, sweet rice flour, potato starch, almond meal, xanthan gum, and salt in a food processor fitted with the steel blade. Blend for 5 seconds. Add butter to the work bowl, and process, using on-and-off pulsing, until mixture resembles coarse meal.

2. Combine egg, egg white, vanilla, and almond extract in a small cup, and whisk well. Drizzle liquid into the work bowl, and pulse about 10 times, or until stiff dough forms. If dough is dry and doesn't come together, add milk by 1-teaspoon amounts, until dough forms a ball.

3. Divide dough in half, and wrap each half in plastic wrap. Press dough into a pancake. Refrigerate dough for 1 hour or until firm, or up to 2 days.

4. Preheat the oven to 350°F. Line two baking sheets with parchment paper or silicon baking mats.

5. Press dough through a cookie press onto the baking sheets. Decorate with sugar sprinkles, candies, and candied cherries as desired.

6. Bake cookies for 10 to 12 minutes, or until edges are brown. Cool cookies for 2 minutes on the baking sheets, and then transfer them with a spatula to cooling racks to cool completely.

Variations
✳ *Substitute lemon oil for the vanilla and almond extracts, and add 1 tablespoon grated lemon zest to the dough.*
✳ *Substitute hazelnut flour for the almond flour.*

> **If you don't have a cookie press, you can still make pretty cookies in interesting shapes. Pipe the dough through a pastry bag fitted with a star tip or a plain tip and pipe the dough into circles like a wreath. Then decorate and bake!**

Linzer Cookies

These are crispy sandwich cookies with a cutout on the top of the cookie through which you see the succulent raspberry jam holding the layers together.

Yield: 2 dozen

Active time: 30 minutes

Start to finish: 1¾ hours, including 1 hour to chill dough

1½ cups white rice flour

¾ cup almond meal

1¼ teaspoons xanthan gum

¾ teaspoon gluten-free baking powder

½ teaspoon salt

¼ pound (1 stick) unsalted butter, softened

¾ cup granulated sugar

1 large egg

1 tablespoon whole milk

¾ teaspoon pure almond extract

Sweet rice flour

¾ cup seedless raspberry jam

⅓ cup confectioners' sugar

1. Combine rice flour, almond meal, xanthan gum, baking powder, and salt in a mixing bowl. Whisk well.

2. Combine butter and sugar in another mixing bowl and beat at low speed with an electric mixer to combine. Increase the speed to high, and beat for 3 to 4 minutes, or until light and fluffy. Add egg, milk, and almond extract, and beat for 1 minute.

3. Slowly add dry ingredients to the butter mixture, and beat until stiff dough forms. Wrap dough in plastic wrap. Press dough into a pancake. Refrigerate dough for 1 hour or until firm, or up to 2 days.

4. Preheat the oven to 350°F. Line two baking sheets with parchment paper or silicon baking mats.

5. Lightly dust a sheet of waxed paper and a rolling pin with sweet rice flour. Roll dough to a thickness of ⅛ inch. Dip a 2-inch flower-shaped cookie cutter in sweet rice flour, and cut out 48 cookies. Remove excess dough, and transfer cookies to the baking sheets. Cut holes with a ¾-inch cutter in the center of 24 cookies. Re-roll excess dough, chilling it for 15 minutes if necessary.

6. Bake cookies for 8 to 10 minutes, or until edges are brown. Cool cookies for 2 minutes on the baking sheets, and then transfer them with a spatula to cooling racks to cool completely.

7. Spread jam on the 24 cookies without the holes. Dust remaining cookies with confectioners' sugar. Place cookies with holes on top of the jam-covered cookies.

Variation
* Substitute melted dark or white chocolate for the jam.

> These cookies are hand-holdable versions of Austria's most famous dessert, the *Linzertorte*. It is believed to have originated in the city of Linz, and written recipes date back to the early eighteenth century. There's always some sort of nut as part of the pastry, and while in Austria it is filled with black currant preserves, in North America we usually use raspberry.

Lemon Cookie Ornaments

These crispy citrus-flavored cookies come from the genre known as "refrigerator cookies." The dough is chilled as a log and then baked as rounds, which makes it easy for mass production.

Yield: 3 dozen

Active time: 20 minutes

Start to finish: 1½ hours, including 1 hour to chill dough

1½ cups white rice flour

1½ cups confectioners' sugar

⅔ cup cornstarch

⅓ cup tapioca starch

1 teaspoon cream of tartar

1 teaspoon baking soda

¾ teaspoon xanthan gum

¼ teaspoon salt

½ pound (2 sticks) unsalted butter, thinly sliced

1 large egg

1 tablespoon whole milk

2 teaspoons grated lemon zest

½ teaspoon lemon oil

Gluten-free sugar sprinkles and candies (optional)

1. Combine rice flour, confectioners' sugar, cornstarch, tapioca starch, cream of tartar, baking soda, xanthan gum, and salt in a food processor fitted with the steel blade. Blend for 5 seconds. Add butter to the work bowl, and process, using on-and-off pulsing, until mixture resembles coarse meal.

2. Combine egg, milk, lemon zest, and lemon oil in a small cup, and whisk well. Drizzle liquid into the work bowl, and pulse about 10 times, or until stiff dough forms. If dough is dry and doesn't come together add additional milk by 1-teaspoon amounts, until dough forms a ball.

3. Place dough on a sheet of waxed paper, and form it into a log 2½-inches in diameter. Refrigerate dough covered in plastic wrap for 1 hour or until firm, or up to 2 days.

4. Preheat the oven to 350°F. Line two baking sheets with parchment paper or silicon baking mats.

5. Cut chilled dough into ¼-inch slices using a sharp serrated knife, and arrange them on the baking sheets. Decorate cookies with sugar crystals, if using.

6. Bake cookies for 10 to 12 minutes, or until edges are brown. Cool cookies for 2 minutes on the baking sheets, and then transfer them with a spatula to cooling racks to cool completely.

Variation

✱ *Substitute lime oil and lime zest for the lemon oil and lemon zest.*

> **You can actually hang these cookies on a small tree. Before baking them, create a small hole at the top with the tip of a paring knife, and make sure the holes have not closed up when the cookies come out of the oven. Loop ribbon through the hole after the cookies cool.**

Peppermint Pinwheels

Combining pink dough flavored with peppermint and white dough creates a delicious cookie that looks harder to make than it is. Peppermint is part and parcel of Christmas and here's another way to enjoy it.

Yield: 2 dozen

Active time: 20 minutes

Start to finish: 3¾ hours, including 3 hours to chill dough

1¼ cups white rice flour

¾ cup confectioners' sugar

¼ cup potato starch

1 teaspoon xanthan gum

½ teaspoon baking soda

¼ teaspoon salt

¼ pound (1 stick) unsalted butter, thinly sliced

1 large egg

1 egg yolk

½ teaspoon peppermint oil or pure peppermint extract

3 to 5 drops red food coloring

1. Combine rice flour, confectioners' sugar, potato starch, xanthan gum, baking soda, and salt in a food processor fitted with the steel blade. Blend for 5 seconds. Add butter to the work bowl, and process, using on-and-off pulsing, until mixture resembles coarse meal.

2. Combine egg and egg yolk in a small cup, and whisk well. Drizzle liquid into the work bowl, and pulse about 10 times, or until stiff dough forms.

3. Remove half of dough from the food processor, and set aside. Add peppermint oil and food coloring to the food processor and process until dough is evenly colored. Wrap each dough in plastic wrap. Press dough into a pancake. Refrigerate dough for 1 hour or until firm, or up to 2 days.

4. Roll out each dough separately into a rectangle approximately ¼-inch thick. Place peppermint dough on top of the white dough, and press together around the edges. Using waxed paper or flexible cutting board underneath as a guide, roll dough into a log shape. Wrap in plastic wrap and refrigerate for 2 hours.

5. Preheat the oven to 350°F. Line two baking sheets with parchment paper or silicon baking mats.

6. Cut chilled dough into slices ¼-inch thick with a sharp serrated knife, and arrange them on the baking sheets.

7. Bake cookies for 10 to 12 minutes, or until edges are brown. Cool cookies for 2 minutes on the baking sheets, and then transfer them with a spatula to cooling racks to cool completely.

Variation

✳ *Substitute green food coloring for the red food coloring, and add ½ cup crushed peppermint candies to the vanilla dough.*

> **Make sure the log is well wrapped in plastic wrap when it's refrigerated the second time. If it's not secure, the dough can dry out and be difficult to cut.**

Ginger Shortbread Fingers

Buttery shortbread comes from the English tradition of baking, and these rich and crispy treats are flavored with spritely candied ginger for an unexpected textural nuance.

Yield: 2 dozen

Active time: 25 minutes

Start to finish: 1¾ hours, including 1 hour to chill dough

2 cups brown rice flour

⅓ cup sweet rice flour

⅓ cup almond meal

1 teaspoon xanthan gum

½ teaspoon salt

½ pound (2 sticks) unsalted butter, softened

⅔ cup firmly packed light brown sugar

½ cup very finely chopped crystallized ginger

½ teaspoon pure vanilla extract

Sweet rice flour

1. Combine rice flour, sweet rice flour, almond meal, xanthan gum, and salt in a mixing bowl. Whisk well.

2. Combine butter and sugar in another mixing bowl and beat at low speed with an electric mixer to combine. Increase the speed to high, and beat for 3 to 4 minutes, or until light and fluffy. Add crystallized ginger and vanilla, and beat for 1 minute.

3. Slowly add dry ingredients to butter mixture, and beat until stiff dough forms. Wrap dough in plastic wrap. Press dough into a pancake. Refrigerate dough for 1 hour or until firm, or up to 2 days.

4. Preheat the oven to 350°F. Line two baking sheets with parchment paper or silicon baking mats.

5. Lightly dust a sheet of waxed paper and a rolling pin with sweet rice flour. Roll dough to a thickness of ½ inch. Cut into rectangles 4 inches long and 1-inch wide. Transfer cookies to the baking sheets. Re-roll excess dough, chilling it for 15 minutes if necessary.

6. Bake cookies for 12 to 15 minutes, or until edges are brown. Cool cookies for 2 minutes on the baking sheets, and then transfer them with a spatula to cooling racks to cool completely.

Variations
* *Add ½ cup dried currants or finely chopped dried apricots to the dough.*
* *Dip one end of cooled cookies into melted white chocolate, and sprinkle with colored sugars.*

> **Crystallized ginger is fresh ginger that is preserved by being candied in sugar syrup. It's then tossed with coarse sugar. It's very expensive in little bottles in the spice aisle, but most whole foods markets sell it in bulk.**

Peanut Butter Chocolate Thumbprint Cookies

Christmas is no time to forget timeless favorites, just dress them up a bit. That's the case with this cookie. The peanut butter dough is topped with a chocolate candy.

Yield: 2 dozen

Active time: 20 minutes

Start to finish: 45 minutes

1¼ cups amaranth flour

¼ cup potato starch

½ teaspoon xanthan gum

½ teaspoon baking soda

Pinch of salt

¾ cup firmly packed light brown sugar

4 tablespoons (½ stick) unsalted butter, softened

½ cup smooth peanut butter

1 large egg

½ teaspoon pure vanilla extract

24 kiss-shaped chocolate candies, unwrapped

1. Preheat the oven to 350°F. Line two baking sheets with parchment paper or silicon baking mats.

2. Combine amaranth flour, potato starch, xanthan gum, baking soda, and salt in a mixing bowl. Whisk well.

3. Combine butter and sugar in another mixing bowl and beat at low speed with an electric mixer to combine. Increase the speed to high, and beat for 3 to 4 minutes, or until light and fluffy. Add peanut butter, egg, and vanilla, and beat for 1 minute.

4. Slowly add dry ingredients to the butter mixture, and beat until stiff dough forms.

5. Roll dough into balls with your hands, and arrange them on the baking sheets. Chill dough if too soft to roll. Press an indentation in the center of each ball with your fingertip, and place one candy in the indentation.

6. Bake cookies for 12 to 14 minutes, or until firm to the touch. Cool cookies for 2 minutes on the baking sheets, and then transfer them with a spatula to cooling racks to cool completely.

Variations

✳ *Substitute sweetened almond butter for the peanut butter, substitute pure almond extract for the vanilla, and substitute ½ cup almond meal for ½ cup of the amaranth flour.*

✳ *Substitute ¾ teaspoon fruit jelly for the candy in the center of the cookies.*

Candied Cherry Walnut Thumbprint Cookies

Coated with crunchy nuts and topped with a brightly colored cherry, these cookies are a favorite with all generations of every family.

Yield: 3 dozen

Active time: 20 minutes

Start to finish: 50 minutes

1½ cups white rice flour

1 cup confectioners' sugar

½ cup cornstarch

1 teaspoon xanthan gum

1 teaspoon cream of tartar

Pinch of salt

½ pound (2 sticks) unsalted butter, cut into thin slices

1 large egg

1 tablespoon whole milk

1 teaspoon pure vanilla extract

1 cup finely chopped walnuts

18 red or green candied cherries, cut in half

1. Preheat the oven to 350°F. Line two baking sheets with parchment paper or silicon baking mats.

2. Combine rice flour, confectioners' sugar, cornstarch, xanthan gum, cream of tartar, and salt in a food processor fitted with the steel blade. Blend for 5 seconds. Add butter to the work bowl, and process, using on-and-off pulsing, until mixture resembles coarse meal.

3. Combine egg, milk, and vanilla in a small cup and whisk well. Drizzle liquid into the work bowl, and pulse about 10 times, or until stiff dough forms. If dough is dry and doesn't come together, add additional milk by 1-teaspoon amounts, until dough forms a ball.

4. Place walnuts on a sheet of waxed paper. Roll dough into balls with your hands, roll them in walnuts, and arrange them on the baking sheets. Chill dough if too soft to roll. Press an indentation in the center of each ball with your fingertip, and place 1 cherry piece in the indentation with the domed side up.

5. Bake cookies for 12 to 14 minutes, or until firm to the touch. Cool cookies for 2 minutes on the baking sheets, and then transfer them with a spatula to cooling racks to cool completely.

Variation
* Substitute ½ teaspoon of strawberry or raspberry jam for the cherry half.

> **Cream of tartar comes from the acid deposited inside wine barrels. It's used in conjunction with baking soda to produce the same chemical reaction as that caused by baking powder.**

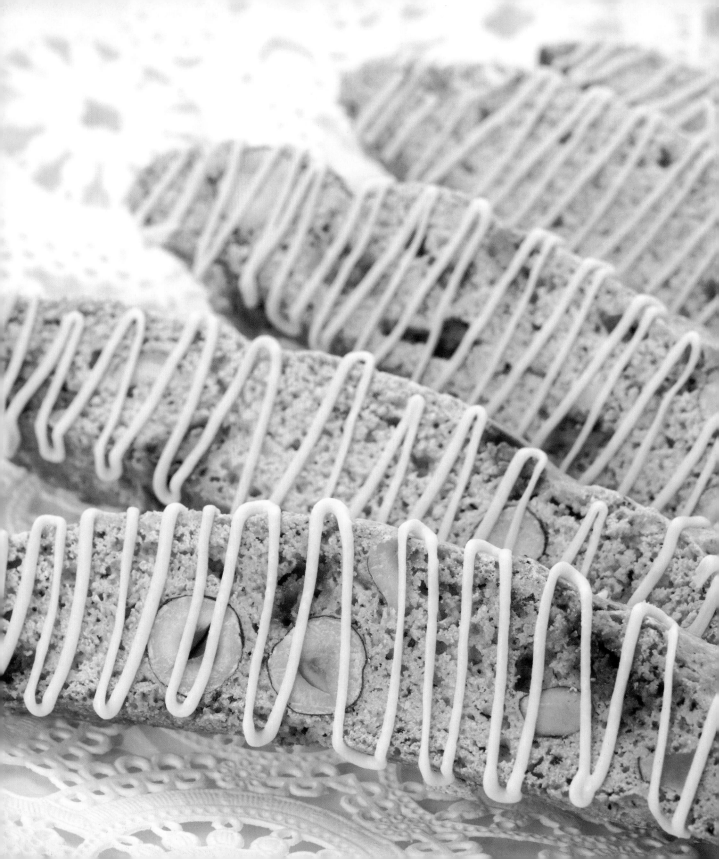

Almond Biscotti

Biscotti are served in Italy all year, not just for the holidays. These deliver their almond flavor in three ways: the nuts, almond meal in the dough, and aromatic almond extract.

Yield: 2 dozen

Active time: 20 minutes

Start to finish: 1¾ hours

1½ cups sliced almonds

½ cup brown rice flour

½ cup almond meal

⅓ cup potato starch

3 tablespoons tapioca starch

1 teaspoon xanthan gum

½ teaspoon gluten-free baking powder

¼ teaspoon salt

¼ pound (1 stick) unsalted butter, softened

1¼ cups confectioners' sugar

2 large eggs

1 teaspoon pure almond extract

1. Preheat the oven to 350°F. Line a baking sheet with parchment paper or a silicon baking mat.

2. Place almonds on a baking sheet, and toast for 5 to 7 minutes, or until lightly browned. Remove nuts from the oven, and set aside.

3. Combine rice flour, almond meal, potato starch, tapioca starch, xanthan gum, baking powder, and salt in a mixing bowl. Whisk well.

4. Combine butter and confectioners' sugar in another mixing bowl and beat at low speed with an electric mixer to combine. Increase the speed to high, and beat for 3 to 4 minutes, or until light and fluffy. Add eggs and almond extract, and beat for 1 minute.

5. Slowly add dry ingredients to the butter mixture, and beat until stiff dough forms. Fold almonds into dough.

6. Form dough into a log 12 inches long and 3 inches wide on the prepared baking sheet. Bake until light golden, about 40 minutes. Cool for 30 minutes.

7. Place log on a cutting board. Cut log on a diagonal into ½- to ¾-inch-thick slices using a sharp, serrated knife. Arrange biscotti, cut side down, on the baking sheet. Bake for 15 minutes, or until pale golden. Transfer biscotti to a rack and cool completely.

Note: If you want soft biscotti rather than hard ones, don't bake them a second time. Bake them for 45 minutes, and then let the log cool for 5 minutes before slicing.

Chocolate Peppermint Biscotti

The combination of chocolate and peppermint is a holiday favorite, and in this case the crispy biscotti are dressed up with a bit of icing and some crushed candies to reinforce the minty freshness.

Yield: 2 dozen

Active time: 25 minutes

Start to finish: 2 hours

1 cup brown rice flour

½ cup unsweetened cocoa powder

⅓ cup potato starch

3 tablespoons tapioca starch

1 teaspoon xanthan gum

½ teaspoon gluten-free baking powder

¼ teaspoon salt

¼ pound (1 stick) unsalted butter, softened

2½ cups confectioners' sugar, divided

2 large eggs

¾ teaspoon peppermint oil or pure peppermint extract, divided

1 (3-ounce) package cream cheese, softened

½ cup crushed peppermint candies

1. Preheat the oven to 350°F. Line a baking sheet with parchment paper or a silicon baking mat.

2. Combine rice flour, cocoa, potato starch, tapioca starch, xanthan gum, baking powder, and salt in a mixing bowl. Whisk well.

3. Combine butter and 1¼ cups confectioners' sugar in another mixing bowl and beat at low speed with an electric mixer to combine. Increase the speed to high, and beat for 3 to 4 minutes, or until light and fluffy. Add eggs and ½ teaspoon peppermint oil, and beat for 1 minute.

4. Slowly add dry ingredients to the butter mixture, and beat until stiff dough forms.

5. Form dough into a log 12 inches long and 3 inches wide on the prepared baking sheet. Bake until light golden, about 40 minutes. Cool for 30 minutes.

6. Place log on a cutting board. Cut log on a diagonal into ½- to ¾-inch-thick slices using a sharp, serrated knife. Arrange biscotti, cut side down, on the baking sheet. Bake for 15 minutes, or until pale golden. Transfer biscotti to a rack and cool completely.

7. For frosting, combine cream cheese, remaining sugar, and remaining peppermint oil in a mixing bowl. Beat at low speed with an electric mixer to combine. Increase the speed to high, and beat for 2 to 3 minutes, or until light and fluffy.

8. Spread frosting on top of thin edge of cookies, and pat peppermint candies on top.

Variation
✱ *Substitute vanilla extract for the peppermint extract, add 1 tablespoon instant espresso powder to the dough, and substitute miniature chocolate chips for the crushed peppermint candies.*

> **If your butter is too hard to blend, do not try to soften it in the microwave oven. A few seconds too long and you've got a melted mess. An easy way to soften butter quickly is to grate it through the large holes of a box grater. It will soften in a matter of minutes at room temperature.**

Holiday Biscotti

Green pistachio nuts and bright red dried cranberries provide holiday colors and wonderfully harmonious flavors in these crispy cookies.

Yield: 2 dozen
Active time: 20 minutes
Start to finish: 1¾ hours

1 cup brown rice flour

⅓ cup potato starch

3 tablespoons tapioca starch

1 teaspoon xanthan gum

½ teaspoon gluten-free baking powder

¼ teaspoon salt

¼ pound (1 stick) unsalted butter, softened

1¼ cups confectioners' sugar

2 large eggs

1 teaspoon pure vanilla extract

¾ cup chopped pistachio nuts

½ cup dried cranberries

1. Preheat the oven to 350°F. Line a baking sheet with parchment paper or a silicon baking mat.

2. Combine rice flour, potato starch, tapioca starch, xanthan gum, baking powder, and salt in a mixing bowl. Whisk well.

3. Combine butter and confectioners' sugar in another mixing bowl and beat at low speed with an electric mixer to combine. Increase the speed to high, and beat for 3 to 4 minutes, or until light and fluffy. Add eggs and vanilla extract, and beat for 1 minute.

4. Slowly add dry ingredients to the butter mixture, and beat until stiff dough forms. Fold pistachios and dried cranberries into dough.

5. Form dough into a log 12 inches long and 3 inches wide on the prepared baking sheet. Bake until light golden, about 40 minutes. Cool for 30 minutes.

6. Place log on a cutting board. Cut log on a diagonal into ½- to ¾-inch-thick slices using a sharp, serrated knife. Arrange biscotti, cut side down, on the baking sheet. Bake for 15 minutes, or until pale golden. Transfer biscotti to a rack and cool completely.

> If you don't have enough cooling racks for cookies you should start them on the rack and then transfer them to sheets of plastic wrap onto which granulated sugar has been sprinkled. The sugar will keep the bottoms from sticking.

Graham Crackers

While graham crackers aren't officially a cookie, let alone a decorative Christmas cookie, being able to make them gluten-free is a gift for the year to someone who must avoid wheat flour. These crackers can be layered with chocolate and marshmallow for S'mores or ground into crumbs for a key lime pie or cheesecake, Layered Chip and Coconut Bars (page 84), or Dried Fruit Coconut Balls (page 124).

Yield: 16 to 20, depending on size

Active time: 20 minutes

Start to finish: 1¾ hours

1½ cups brown rice flour

½ cup cornstarch

⅓ cup firmly packed dark brown sugar

1 teaspoon baking powder

¾ teaspoon xanthan gum

½ teaspoon ground cinnamon

½ teaspoon salt

6 tablespoons (¾ stick) unsalted butter, sliced

5 tablespoons whole milk

¼ cup honey

½ teaspoon pure vanilla extract

Sweet rice flour

1. Combine rice flour, cornstarch, brown sugar, baking powder, xanthan gum, cinnamon, and salt in a food processor fitted with the steel blade. Blend for 5 seconds. Add butter to the work bowl, and process, using on-and-off pulsing, until mixture resembles coarse meal.

2. Combine milk, honey, and vanilla in a small cup, and whisk well. Drizzle liquid into the work bowl, and pulse about 10 times, or until stiff dough forms. If dough is dry and doesn't come together, add additional milk by 1-teaspoon amounts, until dough forms a ball.

3. Divide dough in half, and wrap each half in plastic wrap. Press dough into a pancake. Refrigerate dough for 1 hour or until firm, or up to 2 days.

4. Preheat the oven to 350°F. Line two baking sheets with parchment paper or silicon baking mats.

5. Lightly dust a sheet of waxed paper and a rolling pin with sweet rice flour. Roll each half of dough into a rectangle ¼-inch thick. Transfer dough to the prepared baking sheets, and cut each half into 8 to 10 rectangles with a pizza wheel. Prick dough all over with the tines of a fork.

6. Bake cookies for 15 to 17, or until browned. Allow cookies to cool completely on the cookie sheets placed on a wire cooling rack.

Variations
* *Substitute ground ginger for the ground cinnamon.*
* *Sprinkle cookies with a mixture of ⅓ cup granulated sugar mixed with 1 teaspoon ground cinnamon before baking.*

> **When measuring sticky ingredients such as honey or molasses, first spray the measuring cup with vegetable oil spray. The sticky ingredient will slide right out of the cup.**

CHAPTER 4:

Piles of Perfection:
Drop Cookies

There is nothing about drop cookies that innately say Christmas cookie. They're rarely painted with colored frosting due to their irregular shape, although they can be embellished with tiny candies. But this category contains some of the cookies that make every day a holiday, including our beloved chocolate chip and oatmeal raisin. These are the homey recipes you'll find in this chapter.

While drop cookies do take some time because of individual portioning, this is a task that has traditionally been given over to children once the dough is made. But some guidance is needed because the success of drop cookies depends on mounds of a uniform size. The size not only includes the diameter of the circle, but also its height.

If the cookies are of a uniform size, the difference between chewy cookies and crisp cookies is the baking time. All of these recipes have a range given of a few minutes. If you bake them for the minimum amount of time, you'll have a much moister and chewier cookie than if you let them go for the full baking time, at which point much of the moisture will have evaporated.

In some respects, the word "drop" is inaccurate. While the dough is softer than for rolled cookies, it really doesn't drop onto the baking sheets without some coaxing. There are two ways to accomplish this task: another spoon or a finger. If using the "two spoon method," spray both spoons with vegetable oil spray first to make it easier to slide the dough off with the other spoon. Here are some other tips for making drop cookies:

- Cool your cookie sheets by running the back under cold water between batches. Placing dough on a warm cookie sheet makes the cookies flatten.
- Take note of how far apart the mounds of cookie dough should be placed on the baking sheet. Some cookies spread far more than others.
- Rotate the cookie sheets midway through the baking time if using two sheets. Even if baking with a convection fan, cookies on an upper rack brown more quickly than those on a lower rack.
- Always allow cookies to cool for 2 minutes on the baking sheets before transferring them to cooling racks.

Note: Unless otherwise noted, use these directions for storing cookies in this chapter: keep cookies in an airtight container, layered between sheets of waxed paper or parchment, at room temperature for up to 5 days. Cookies can also be frozen for up to two months. Do not freeze cookies if decorated.

Snowball Cookies

These are sometimes called Mexican Wedding Cookies. They are crispy and buttery and dusted in confectioners' sugar as a decoration.

Yield: 3 dozen

Active time: 15 minutes

Start to finish: 30 minutes

1 cup chopped pecans

1½ cups white rice flour

¼ cup potato starch

¼ cup sweet rice flour

½ teaspoon xanthan gum

½ teaspoon salt

½ pound (2 sticks) unsalted butter

1½ cups confectioners' sugar, divided

1 teaspoon pure vanilla extract

1. Preheat the oven to 350°F. Line two baking sheets with parchment paper or silicon baking mats. Place pecans on a baking sheet, and toast for 5 to 7 minutes, or until lightly browned. Set aside. Reduce the oven temperature to 325°F.

2. Combine rice flour, potato starch, sweet rice flour, xanthan gum, and salt in a mixing bowl. Whisk well.

3. Combine butter and 1 cup confectioners' sugar in another mixing bowl and beat at low speed with an electric mixer to combine. Increase the speed to high, and beat for 3 to 4 minutes, or until light and fluffy. Add vanilla, and beat for 1 minute.

4. Slowly add dry ingredients to the butter mixture, and beat until stiff dough forms. Fold in pecans.

5. Form dough into 1-tablespoon mounds on the baking sheets, 1½ inches apart. Bake cookies for 15 to 20 minutes, or until lightly brown. Cool for 2 minutes on the baking sheets.

6. Place remaining ½ cup confectioners' sugar in a shallow bowl. Dip tops of cookies in sugar, and then cool completely on a cooling rack.

Variations
* *Substitute sweetened coconut for the pecans.*
* *Substitute 1 tablespoon grated orange zest for the vanilla.*

> To meet the standards set by the Food and Drug Administration, pure vanilla extract must contain about 1 pound vanilla beans per gallon; that's why it's about twice as expensive as imitation extract. It's clearly worth the money, considering how little you use. Look at the labels carefully before you buy.

Brazilian Sugar Cookies

Called Biscoitos de Maizena *in Portuguese, these cookies take the name of Brazil's leading brand of cornstarch. They are very quick to make, and they almost melt in your mouth.*

Yield: 3 dozen

Active time: 15 minutes

Start to finish: 30 minutes

2½ cups cornstarch

1¼ cups granulated sugar

½ teaspoon salt

½ pound (2 sticks) unsalted butter, thinly sliced

1 large egg

1 large egg yolk

¾ teaspoon pure vanilla extract

1. Preheat the oven to 375°F. Line two baking sheets with parchment paper or silicon baking mats.

2. Combine cornstarch, sugar, and salt in a food processor fitted with the steel blade. Blend for 5 seconds. Add butter to the work bowl, and process, using on-and-off pulsing, until mixture resembles coarse meal.

3. Combine egg, egg yolk, and vanilla in a small cup, and whisk well. Drizzle liquid into the work bowl, and pulse about 10 times, or until stiff dough forms. If dough is dry and doesn't come together, add milk by 1-teaspoon amounts, until dough forms a ball.

4. Form 1-tablespoon amounts of dough into balls, and transfer balls to the prepared baking sheets, leaving 2 inches of space between balls. Flatten balls with the tines of a fork to make a crosshatch pattern.

5. Bake for 7 to 10 minutes, or until lightly brown. Cool cookies on the baking sheets for 2 minutes, and then transfer to a wire rack to cool completely.

Variation

✳ *Substitute pure almond extract for the vanilla, and substitute ½ cup almond meal for ½ cup of the cornstarch.*

> Brown & Polson in Paisley, Scotland, have been selling cornstarch, which they call corn flour, since 1840, and a man named Orlando Jones patented it in the U.S. a year later. During the "Emergency," as the Irish called World War II, a special act was passed setting the maximum price for Brown & Polson Corn flour in Ireland at 5 pence for a ¼-pound package.

Cornmeal Dried Fruit Cookies

These are really unusual cookies, made with cornmeal and loaded with succulent dried fruit steeped in rum. I serve these at Thanksgiving, too.

Yield: 3 dozen

Active time: 15 minutes

Start to finish: 40 minutes

¼ cup golden raisins

¼ cup dried cranberries

¼ cup dried cherries

¼ cup rum

1½ cups cornmeal

1½ cups cornstarch

¾ cup granulated sugar

1 teaspoon gluten-free baking powder

½ teaspoon xanthan gum

½ teaspoon salt

¼ pound (1 stick) unsalted butter, sliced

2 large eggs

2 tablespoons whole milk

1 tablespoon grated orange zest

½ teaspoon pure vanilla extract

1. Preheat the oven to 350°F. Line two baking sheets with parchment paper or silicon baking mats. Combine golden raisins, dried cranberries, dried cherries, and rum in a small mixing bowl, and toss to coat fruit with rum.

2. Combine cornmeal, cornstarch, sugar, baking powder, xanthan gum, and salt in a food processor fitted with the steel blade. Blend for 5 seconds. Add butter to the work bowl, and process, using on-and-off pulsing, until mixture resembles coarse meal.

3. Combine eggs, milk, orange zest, and vanilla in a small cup, and whisk well. Drizzle liquid into the work bowl, and pulse about 10 times, or until stiff dough forms. If dough is dry and doesn't come together, add additional milk by 1-teaspoon amounts, until dough forms a ball.

4. Scrape dough into a mixing bowl, and stir in fruit and whatever rum remains in the bowl.

5. Drop dough by 1-tablespoon portions onto the prepared baking sheets, 2 inches apart. Bake cookies for 20 to 25 minutes, or until cookies are dry. Cool cookies for 2 minutes on the baking sheets, and then transfer to a wire rack to cool completely.

Variations
* *Substitute ⅓ cup chopped walnuts, toasted in a 350°F oven for 5 to 7 minutes, for some of the dried fruits.*
* *Substitute chopped candied citrus peels and candied cherries for the dried fruits.*

> One way to save time when you need to grate a lot of citrus zest is to use a vegetable peeler to separate the colored zest from the bitter white pith beneath it. Then place the strips in a mini-food processor and it will be finely chopped in seconds.

Peanut Butter Cookies

Every cookie collection needs to include one for peanut butter, which kids love and brings out the kid in every adult, too. This gluten-free version is especially tasty because of the brown sugar.

Yield: 2 to 3 dozen

Active time: 20 minutes

Start to finish: 35 minutes

1 cup brown rice flour

¼ cup tapioca flour

¼ cup cornstarch

1¼ teaspoons gluten-free baking powder

½ teaspoon xanthan gum

½ teaspoon salt

¼ pound (1 stick) unsalted butter, softened

1 cup peanut butter (either smooth or chunky)

½ cup granulated sugar

½ cup firmly packed dark brown sugar

1 large egg

1 large egg yolk

½ teaspoon pure vanilla extract

1. Preheat the oven to 375°F. Line two baking sheets with parchment paper or silicon baking mats.

2. Combine rice flour, tapioca flour, cornstarch, baking powder, xanthan gum, and salt in a mixing bowl. Whisk well.

3. Combine butter, peanut butter, granulated sugar, and brown sugar in another mixing bowl and beat at low speed with an electric mixer to combine. Increase the speed to high, and beat for 3 to 4 minutes, or until light and fluffy. Add egg, egg yolk, and vanilla, and beat for 1 minute.

4. Slowly add dry ingredients to the butter mixture, and beat until stiff dough forms.

5. Form 1-tablespoon amounts of dough into balls, and transfer balls to the prepared baking sheets, leaving 2 inches of space between balls. Flatten balls with the tines of a fork to make a crosshatch pattern.

6. Bake for 8 to 10 minutes, or until golden brown. Cool cookies on the baking sheets for 2 minutes, and then transfer to a wire rack to cool completely.

Variations
* *Add 1 cup chocolate chips to the dough before baking.*
* *Substitute almond butter or cashew butter for the peanut butter.*

> George Washington Carver, an educator at the Tuskegee Institute in Alabama, was an avid promoter of peanuts as a replacement for the region's cotton crop, which had been severely damaged by the boll weevil. In his 1916 Research Bulletin called *How to Grow the Peanut and 105 Ways of Preparing it for Human Consumption*, he included three recipes for peanut cookies calling for crushed/chopped peanuts as an ingredient. It was not until the early 1920s that peanut butter was listed as an ingredient in cookies.

Piña Colada Oatmeal Cookies

The tropical combination of pineapple, coconut, and rum is a winner whether it's in a cookie or in a glass. These cookies contain lots of healthful oats, too.

Yield: 4 dozen

Active time: 20 minutes

Start to finish: 40 minutes

1½ cups unsweetened flaked coconut

1¼ cups gluten-free oat flour

½ cup tapioca starch

¼ cup brown rice flour

1½ teaspoons baking soda

1 teaspoon xanthan gum

½ teaspoon salt

1½ cups firmly packed light brown sugar

1½ cups (3 sticks) unsalted butter, softened

2 large eggs

1 teaspoon rum extract

3 cups gluten-free rolled oats

1 cup chopped dried pineapple

1. Preheat the oven to 350°F. Line two baking sheets with parchment paper or silicon baking mats. Place coconut on a baking sheet, and toast for 5 to 7 minutes, or until brown. Set aside.

2. Combine oat flour, tapioca starch, rice flour, baking soda, xanthan gum, and salt in a mixing bowl. Whisk well.

3. Combine brown sugar and butter in another mixing bowl and beat at low speed with an electric mixer to combine. Increase the speed to high, and beat for 3 to 4 minutes, or until light and fluffy. Add eggs and rum extract, and beat for 1 minute.

4. Slowly add dry ingredients to the butter mixture, and beat until stiff dough forms. Stir in coconut, oats, and pineapple.

5. Drop 1-tablespoon amounts of dough onto the prepared baking sheets, leaving 2 inches of space between balls. Flatten mounds slightly with the bottom of a glass dipped into rice flour.

6. Bake for 10 to 12 minutes, or until lightly brown. Cool cookies on the baking sheets for 2 minutes, and then transfer to a wire rack to cool completely.

Variation

* *Substitute raisins or chopped dried apricots for the dried pineapple.*

> You can use packaged gluten-free oat flour in this recipe or you can easily prepare your own by grinding oats in a clean coffee grinder. To prepare 1¼ cups oat flour, you'll need about 1½ cups of rolled oats. Grind them in small batches.

Chocolate Chip Cookies

Here's everyone's favorite cookie regardless of season, and to dress them up for Christmas, substitute red and green candy-coated chocolate candies for the classic chips.

Yield: 2 to 3 dozen
Active time: 15 minutes
Start to finish: 30 minutes

¾ cup chopped walnuts

1¼ cups brown rice flour

½ cup sweet rice flour

¼ cup cornstarch

1 teaspoon baking soda

½ teaspoon xanthan gum

½ teaspoon salt

12 tablespoons (1½ sticks) unsalted butter, softened

1 cup firmly packed light brown sugar

2 large eggs

1 teaspoon pure vanilla extract

1 (12-ounce) bag bittersweet chocolate chips

1. Preheat the oven to 350°F. Line two baking sheets with parchment paper or silicon baking mats. Place walnuts on a baking sheet, and toast for 5 to 7 minutes, or until lightly browned.

2. Combine brown rice flour, sweet rice flour, cornstarch, baking soda, xanthan gum, and salt in a mixing bowl. Whisk well.

3. Combine sugar and butter and in another mixing bowl and beat at low speed with an electric mixer. Increase the speed to high, and beat for 3 to 4 minutes, or until light and fluffy. Add eggs and vanilla, and beat for 1 minute.

4. Slowly add dry ingredients to the butter mixture, and beat until stiff dough forms. Stir in walnuts and chocolate chips.

5. Drop 1-tablespoon amounts of dough onto the prepared baking sheets, leaving 2 inches of space between cookies.

6. Bake for 10 to 12 minutes, or until lightly brown. Cool cookies on the baking sheets for 2 minutes, and then transfer to a wire rack to cool completely.

Variation
✳ *Substitute macadamia nuts for walnuts and substitute white chocolate chips for bittersweet chocolate chips.*

> The chocolate chip cookie was developed in 1930 by Ruth Graves Wakefield, owner of the Toll House Inn in Whitman, Massachusetts. The restaurant's popularity was not just due to its home-cooked–style meals; her policy was to give diners a whole extra helping of their entrées to take home with them and a serving of her homemade cookies for dessert.

Mexican Chocolate Cookies

Ibarra is the famous brand of Mexican chocolate flavored with cinnamon and ground almonds, which is sold in blocks and used for making hot chocolate. Those flavor nuances are part of these cookies, too.

Yield: 2 dozen

Active time: 20 minutes

Start to finish: 40 minutes

1½ cups blanched almonds

3 cups confectioners' sugar, divided

¾ cup Dutch-process cocoa powder

1 teaspoon ground cinnamon

½ teaspoon salt

5 ounces bittersweet chocolate, chopped

4 large egg whites, at room temperature

½ teaspoon pure almond extract

1. Preheat oven to 350°F. Line two baking sheets with parchment paper or silicon baking mats. Place almonds on a baking sheet, and toast for 5 to 7 minutes, or until lightly browned.

2. Decrease the oven temperature to 325°F. Place almonds and 1 cup confectioners' sugar in a food processor fitted with the steel blade, and chop almonds finely using on-and-off pulsing.

3. Scrape almond mixture into a mixing bowl, and add remaining sugar, cocoa powder, cinnamon, and salt. Whisk well, and stir in chocolate, egg whites, and almond extract. Stir well.

4. Drop dough by heaping 1-tablespoon portions onto the prepared baking sheets, 2 inches apart. Bake cookies for 20 to 25 minutes, or until cookies are dry. Cool cookies for 2 minutes on the baking sheets, and then transfer to a wire rack to cool completely.

Variation
✽ *Substitute walnuts for the almonds and vanilla extract for the almond extract. Omit the cinnamon.*

> **Cinnamon is the inner bark of a tropical evergreen tree that's harvested during the rainy season and then allowed to dry. At that time it's sold as sticks or ground. What we call cinnamon is cassia cinnamon, and there's also a Ceylon cinnamon that is less pungent.**

Chocolate-Dipped Florentines

These traditional Italian cookies are crispy and sophisticated. The nutty cookies are very flat once baked, and then the edges are dipped in chocolate to make them richer.

Yield: 5 dozen
Active time: 25 minutes
Start to finish: 1 hour

6 ounces sliced, blanched almonds (about 2 cups)

2 tablespoons white rice flour

1 tablespoon cornstarch

⅛ teaspoon xanthan gum

¼ teaspoon salt

¾ cup granulated sugar

2 tablespoons heavy cream

2 tablespoons light corn syrup

5 tablespoons unsalted butter

½ teaspoon pure vanilla extract

6 ounces bittersweet chocolate, chopped

1. Combine almonds, rice flour, cornstarch, xanthan gum, and salt in a food processor fitted with the steel blade. Chop finely using on-and-off pulsing. Scrape mixture into a mixing bowl.

2. Combine sugar, cream, corn syrup, and butter in a small saucepan. Bring to a boil over medium heat, stirring frequently to dissolve sugar. Boil for 2 minutes, stirring constantly. Remove the pan from the heat, and stir in the vanilla.

3. Pour liquid over the almond mixture, and stir to combine evenly. Set aside to cool for 30 minutes, or until cool enough to handle.

4. Preheat the oven to 350°F. Line two baking sheets with parchment paper or silicon baking mats.

5. Place rounded teaspoons of dough onto the prepared baking sheets, allowing 3 inches between mounds. Bake for 10 to 12 minutes, or until golden brown. Cool cookies on the baking sheets for 2 minutes, and then transfer to a wire rack to cool completely. Repeat with remaining cookies, as necessary.

6. Place chocolate in a small microwave-safe bowl, and melt at medium (50 percent power) at 30-second intervals until chocolate is melted and smooth.

7. Holding each cookie in the center between your thumb and index finger, dip edges of cookies into chocolate, and place cookies back on racks until chocolate sets. Reheat chocolate as necessary.

Variation
* *Substitute chopped hazelnuts for the almonds.*

One of the additional health benefits of chocolate is that it has been found to contain *catechins*—some of the same antioxidants found in green tea. The catechins attack free radicals, which damage cells and are thought to lead to cancer and heart disease. So eating chocolate may help prevent heart disease and cancer, as long as it's eaten in small quantities.

Almond Cookies

These cookies are reminiscent of those served in Chinese restaurants, with a really intense almond flavor.

Yield: 2 dozen
Active time: 15 minutes
Start to finish: 35 minutes

¾ cup amaranth flour

½ cup almond meal

¼ cup cornstarch

½ teaspoon xanthan gum

½ teaspoon baking soda

¼ teaspoon salt

½ cup smooth almond butter

4 tablespoons (½ stick) unsalted butter, softened

½ cup granulated sugar

½ cup firmly packed light brown sugar

1 large egg

1 teaspoon pure almond extract

24 blanched almonds

1. Preheat the oven to 350°F. Line two baking sheets with parchment paper or silicon baking mats.

2. Combine amaranth flour, almond meal, cornstarch, xanthan gum, baking soda, and salt in a mixing bowl. Whisk well.

3. Combine almond butter, butter, granulated sugar, and brown sugar in another mixing bowl and beat at low speed with an electric mixer to combine. Increase the speed to high, and beat for 3 to 4 minutes, or until light and fluffy. Add egg and almond extract, and beat for 1 minute.

4. Slowly add dry ingredients to the butter mixture, and beat until stiff dough forms.

5. Form 1-tablespoon amounts of dough into balls, and transfer balls to the prepared baking sheets, leaving 2 inches of space between balls. Flatten balls with the bottom of a glass dipped into amaranth flour to a thickness of ⅓-inch. Press 1 almond into the center of each cookie.

6. Bake for 10 to 12 minutes, or until lightly brown. Cool cookies on the baking sheets for 2 minutes, and then transfer to a wire rack to cool completely.

Variation
* *Substitute cashew butter for the almond butter, vanilla extract for the almond extract, and press cashews into the cookies before baking.*

Brown sugar is granulated sugar mixed with molasses, and the darker the color, the more pronounced the molasses flavor. If a recipe calls for dark brown sugar, and you only have light brown sugar, add 2 tablespoons molasses per ½ cup sugar to replicate the taste.

Triple Chocolate Hazelnut Cookies

These cookies are one of my favorite recipes in this book. They deliver an incredibly rich chocolate flavor, and the hazelnuts add a tantalizing crunch.

Yield: 3 to 4 dozen
Active time: 20 minutes
Start to finish: 40 minutes

1½ cups skinned hazelnuts

½ pound bittersweet chocolate

3 tablespoons unsalted butter

2 tablespoons brown rice flour

2 tablespoons unsweetened cocoa powder

1 tablespoon cornstarch

¼ teaspoon gluten-free baking powder

¼ teaspoon xanthan gum

¼ teaspoon salt

2 large eggs

½ cup granulated sugar

2 tablespoons Frangelico or other hazelnut-flavored liqueur

½ teaspoon pure vanilla extract

1 cup bittersweet chocolate chips

1. Preheat the oven to 350°F. Line two baking sheets with parchment paper or silicon baking mats. Place hazelnuts on a baking sheet, and toast for 5 to 7 minutes, or until lightly browned.

2. Break chocolate into pieces no larger than a lima bean. Either chop chocolate in a food processor fitted with a steel blade using on-and-off pulsing, or place it in a heavy re-sealable plastic bag, and smash it with the back of a heavy skillet.

3. Melt chocolate and butter in a heavy saucepan over low heat, stirring frequently until the mixture is melted and smooth. Remove the pan from the heat, and set aside for 5 to 7 minutes to cool. This can also be done in a microwave oven.

4. Combine rice flour, cocoa, cornstarch, baking powder, xanthan gum, and salt in a mixing bowl. Whisk well.

5. Combine eggs, sugar, Frangelico, and vanilla in a mixing bowl. Beat at high speed with an electric mixer for 1 minute. Beat in the cooled chocolate mixture, and then the dry ingredients. Fold in nuts and chocolate chips.

6. Drop dough by 1-tablespoon portions onto the prepared baking sheets, leaving 1½ inches of space between cookies.

7. Bake for 10 to 12 minutes, or until tops are dry. Cool cookies on the baking sheets for 2 minutes, and then transfer to a wire rack to cool completely.

Variations
✳ *Add 1 tablespoon instant espresso powder to the chocolate and butter mixture for mocha cookies.*
✳ *Add ½ teaspoon ground cinnamon to the dough.*
✳ *Substitute white chocolate chips for the bittersweet chocolate chips.*

> **Gluten-free cookie dough is frequently softer than dough made with wheat flour both because the substitutes don't create gluten, and because usually more butter is added. If you have problems forming balls with the dough, just refrigerate it until it's stiff enough to roll.**

CHAPTER 5:

Luscious Layers:
Bar Cookies and Brownies

There's no question that bar cookies are the quickest and easiest cookies to make. After the batter or dough is mixed it's baked in one pan, and then cut into pieces. You're done. How many cookies each batch makes depends on how large the pieces are that you cut, and for Christmas, when you're baking any number of different cookies, I suggest cutting the bars into no more than two-inch pieces.

There's no need to spend time chilling the dough because it's not going to be rolled, and there's no need to take the time to form individual portions as you do for drop cookies. Bar cookie recipes do require a longer baking time, but while they're in the oven you can be trimming your tree.

A subset of bar cookies is ever-popular brownies and their first cousin, blondies. You'll find a good range of those recipes in this chapter, too.

One downside of bar cookies at Christmas, however, is that they usually don't have the visual appeal of decorated sugar cookies or whimsical gingerbread people. My suggestion is to cut them into very small bites, and present them in small paper cups as miniatures. This approach also increases the batch size from twelve or sixteen larger cookies to at least two dozen.

Another way to dress them up is by cutting them into shapes other than squares and rectangles. Diamond-shaped cookies are pretty, and if you cut the bars with a round biscuit cutter you have all the tiny bits between the cookies as a treat for the cook!

Slicing and Dicing Tips

How and when you cut bar cookies depends on the recipe. With most, you allow the pan to cool completely on a wire cooling rack, and then cut them, but there are also recipes that benefit from being chilled before being sliced.

A sharp, serrated knife is the best tool to use, although the knife can damage the pan. Lining the baking pan with heavy-duty aluminum foil, allowing the foil to come up high enough that you can fold it over makes it possible to remove the bar cookies from the pan, and cut them on a cutting board. It also means you don't have to wash the pan. Line the pan, pressing the foil into all the crevices and edges, and then treat it as dictated in the recipe, either just greased or greased and dusted with sweet rice flour.

The key to successful slicing is to proceed *slowly*. If you cut cookies too quickly, it can cause the edges to fracture and you're left with crumbs instead of slices. If slicing them in the pan, begin by creating space in the pan by removing the four edges, which are never as attractive. Cut around about ½-inch into the pan, and then remove those thin slices and consider them a treat. Then work from alternate sides. Depending on the cookie, it's frequently easier to cut a long slice and then divide it out of the pan.

Alternate tools for successfully slicing bar cookies are a curved pizza rocker or a traditional pizza wheel. Only use the wheel on thin cookies, but the rounded edge of the rocker makes it perfect for all cookies.

Note: Unless otherwise directed, you can keep the cookies in this chapter in an airtight container, layered between sheets of waxed paper or parchment, at room temperature for up to 5 days. Do not freeze.

Almond Bars

Almond paste gives these dense and chewy cookies an intense almond flavor, balanced by the crunch provided by the almonds on the top.

Yield: 2 to 3 dozen

Active time: 15 minutes

Start to finish: 1 hour

¾ cup brown rice flour

¾ cup confectioners' sugar

½ cup potato starch

½ teaspoon xanthan gum

½ teaspoon baking soda

½ teaspoon salt

12 tablespoons (1½ sticks) unsalted butter, sliced

⅔ cup firmly packed almond paste

1 large egg

1 tablespoon whole milk

1 teaspoon pure almond extract

1 large egg white

1 cup sliced almonds

1. Preheat the oven to 350°F. Grease a 9 x 9-inch baking pan.

2. Combine rice flour, confectioners' sugar, potato starch, xanthan gum, baking soda, and salt in a food processor fitted with the steel blade. Blend for 5 seconds. Add butter and almond paste to the work bowl, and process until mixture resembles coarse meal.

3. Combine egg, milk, and almond extract in a small cup, and whisk well. Drizzle liquid into the work bowl, and pulse about 10 times, or until stiff dough forms. If dough is dry and doesn't come together, add additional milk by 1-teaspoon amounts, until dough forms a ball.

4. Press dough into the prepared pan. Whisk egg white in a small cup and spread over dough. Pat almonds evenly onto dough.

5. Bake for 35 to 40 minutes, or until top is golden. Cool completely in the pan on a cooling rack, then cut into pieces.

Variation
✳ *Substitute chocolate chips for the almonds, and omit the egg white.*

Be careful when purchasing almond paste. Solo brand, which is widely available, is gluten-free, but some brands use wheat starch, which is clearly on the label. So look carefully before you buy it.

Cranberry Nut Bars

These chewy bars are the epitome of New England; they join crispy walnuts and succulent dried cranberries, both of which are native to the region.

Yield: 3 to 4 dozen
Active time: 20 minutes
Start to finish: 45 minutes

¾ cup chopped walnuts

1 cup brown rice flour

⅓ cup potato starch

¼ cup tapioca starch

1 teaspoon gluten-free baking powder

¾ teaspoon xanthan gum

¼ teaspoon salt

¼ pound (1 stick) unsalted butter, softened

1¼ cups firmly packed light brown sugar

2 large eggs

½ teaspoon pure vanilla extract

1 cup chopped fresh or frozen cranberries

1. Preheat the oven to 350°F, and grease a 9 x 13-inch baking pan. Place walnuts on a cookie sheet, and toast for 5 to 7 minutes, or until lightly browned.

2. Combine rice flour, potato starch, tapioca starch, baking powder, xanthan gum, and salt in a mixing bowl. Whisk well.

3. Combine butter and brown sugar in another mixing bowl and beat at low speed with an electric mixer to combine. Increase the speed to high, and beat for 3 to 4 minutes, or until light and fluffy. Add eggs, one at a time, and vanilla, and beat for 1 minute.

4. Slowly add dry ingredients to the butter mixture, and beat well combined. Fold walnuts and cranberries into dough. Spread dough evenly in the prepared pan.

5. Bake for 20 to 25 minutes, or until brown. Cool completely in the pan on a cooling rack, then cut into pieces.

Variation
✳ *Substitute chopped almonds for the walnuts, and substitute pure almond extract for the vanilla.*

The cranberry, along with the blueberry and Concord grape, is one of North America's three native fruits that are still commercially grown. Native Americans, who discovered the wild berry's versatility as a food, fabric dye, and healing agent, were the first to use cranberries.

Oatmeal Pumpkin Nut Bars

This is a homey cookie with a streusel topping flavored with the same aromatic spices used in pumpkin pie. And there's a caramel layer in the center that adds even more richness.

Yield: 3 to 4 dozen

Active time: 20 minutes

Start to finish: 1 hour

1 cup chopped pecans

2 cups gluten-free rolled oats

1½ cups brown rice flour

½ cup potato starch

1½ cups firmly packed light brown sugar

1½ teaspoons ground cinnamon

1 teaspoon baking soda

1 teaspoon xanthan gum

1 teaspoon ground ginger

½ teaspoon salt

½ pound (2 sticks) unsalted butter, melted

1 cup solid-pack canned pumpkin

1 teaspoon pure vanilla extract

7 ounces (½ of 14-ounce bag) caramels, unwrapped

2 tablespoons whole milk

1. Preheat the oven to 350°F. Line a 9 x 13-inch baking pan with heavy-duty aluminum foil, allowing the sides to be long and wrapped around the sides of the pan. Grease the foil. Place pecans on a baking sheet, and toast for 5 to 7 minutes, or until lightly browned.

2. Combine nuts, oats, rice flour, potato starch, brown sugar, cinnamon, baking soda, xanthan gum, ginger, and salt in a mixing bowl, and whisk well. Add butter, and stir until mixture resembles a coarse meal. Reserve ½ of mixture.

3. Add pumpkin and vanilla to mixture still remaining in the mixing bowl. Press dough into the bottom of the prepared pan.

4. Combine caramels and milk in a microwavable bowl, and microwave on high (100 percent power) for 1-minute intervals until caramels are completely melted. Place dollops of caramel on top of dough, and spread into an even layer. Sprinkle reserved mixture over caramel.

5. Bake for 30 to 35 minutes, or until lightly browned. Cool completely in the pan on a cooling rack, then cut into pieces.

Variation
✳ *Substitute apple pie spice for the cinnamon and ginger, and substitute walnuts for the pecans.*

> **Be careful when shopping for pumpkin in the supermarket. Right next to the solid-pack pumpkin are cans of pumpkin pie filling, which are already sweetened and spiced, but most importantly, contain gluten.**

Caramel Pecan Bars

These rich and gooey cookies are like a pecan pie you can hold in your fingers. They are drawn from the Southern tradition, and every generation loves them.

Yield: 2 to 3 dozen
Active time: 20 minutes
Start to finish: 1 hour

½ **pound pecan halves**
¼ **cup brown rice flour**
¼ **cup confectioners' sugar**
¼ **cup sweet rice flour**
¼ **cup potato starch**
¼ **cup almond meal**
½ **teaspoon xanthan gum**
¼ **teaspoon salt**
½ **pound (2 sticks) unsalted butter, sliced, divided**
1 **large egg**
½ **teaspoon pure vanilla extract**
¼ **teaspoon pure almond extract**
¾ **cup firmly packed light brown sugar**
¼ **cup light corn syrup**
¼ **cup heavy cream**

1. Preheat the oven to 375°F. Line a 9 x 9-inch baking pan with heavy-duty aluminum foil, allowing the sides to be long and wrapped around the sides of the pan. Grease the foil. Place pecans on a baking sheet, and toast for 5 to 7 minutes, or until lightly browned.

2. Combine rice flour, confectioners' sugar, sweet rice flour, potato starch, almond meal, xanthan gum, and salt in a food processor fitted with the steel blade. Blend for 5 seconds. Add ½ of butter to the bowl, and process, using on-and-off pulsing, until mixture resembles coarse meal.

3. Combine egg, vanilla, and almond extract in a small cup, and whisk well. Drizzle liquid into the work bowl, and pulse about 10 times, or until stiff dough forms. If dough is dry and doesn't come together, add milk by 1-teaspoon amounts, until dough forms a ball.

4. Transfer dough to prepared pan. Using floured fingers and an offset spatula, press dough firmly into the bottom and ¾ inch up the sides. Freeze until firm, about 15 minutes. Prick dough on the bottom of the pan with the tines of a fork. Bake crust for 10 to 12 minutes, or until lightly browned.

5. While crust bakes, prepare topping. Combine remaining butter, brown sugar, and corn syrup in a saucepan, and bring to a boil over high heat, whisking constantly. Boil for 2 minutes. Remove the pan from the heat, and stir in cream and pecans.

6. Spoon topping over crust, smoothing the top with a spatula. Bake for 20 to 22 minutes, or until topping is bubbling and dark brown. Cool completely in the pan on a cooling rack. Remove from the pan by pulling up on the sides of the foil, and cut into small squares.

Variations
✳ *Substitute maple sugar for the light brown sugar, substitute pure maple syrup for the corn syrup, and substitute walnuts for the pecans.*
✳ *Add ½ cup dried currants to the topping.*

> **The reason why the crust in this recipe is pricked with a fork is to prevent shrinkage while it bakes. Even without gluten, the dough has a tendency to shrink when heated and the liquid evaporates.**

Lemon Squares

I've been making these lemon squares since I was a child, and they remain at the top of my list. This is also a great last-minute recipe since most of us have a lemon or two in the house, along with basic baking ingredients.

Yield: 2 to 3 dozen
Active time: 15 minutes
Start to finish: 1 hour

¼ cup brown rice flour

¼ cup confectioners' sugar

¼ cup sweet rice flour

¼ cup potato starch

¼ cup almond meal

½ teaspoon xanthan gum

¼ teaspoon salt

¼ pound (1 stick) unsalted butter, sliced

3 large eggs, divided

½ teaspoon pure vanilla extract

1 cup granulated sugar

1 tablespoon cornstarch

⅓ cup freshly squeezed lemon juice

1 tablespoon grated lemon zest

Confectioners' sugar for dusting

1. Preheat the oven to 350°F. Line a 9 x 9-inch baking pan with heavy-duty aluminum foil, allowing the sides to be long and wrapped around the sides of the pan. Grease the foil.

2. Combine rice flour, confectioners' sugar, sweet rice flour, potato starch, almond meal, xanthan gum, and salt in a food processor fitted with the steel blade. Blend for 5 seconds. Add butter to the work bowl, and process, using on-and-off pulsing, until mixture resembles coarse meal.

3. Combine 1 egg and vanilla in a small cup, and whisk well. Drizzle liquid into the work bowl, and pulse about 10 times, or until stiff dough forms. If dough is dry and doesn't come together add milk by 1-teaspoon amounts, until dough forms a ball.

4. Press dough into the bottom of the prepared pan. Bake crust for 20 minutes, or until lightly browned.

5. While crust bakes, prepare topping. Combine remaining 2 eggs, sugar, cornstarch, lemon juice, and lemon zest in a mixing bowl. Beat at medium speed with an electric mixer for 1 minute, or until well blended.

6. Pour topping over crust and bake for 20 minutes, or until barely brown. Custard should still be soft. Dust with confectioners' sugar. Cool completely in the pan on a cooling rack, then cut into pieces.

Note: The cookies can be refrigerated for up to 1 week, tightly covered.

Variations
✻ *Substitute lime juice and lime zest for the lemon ingredients, and add 1 or 2 drops of green food coloring to the topping.*
✻ *Instead of dusting the bars with confectioners' sugar, heat some seedless raspberry jam and glaze them with it.*

> Confectioners' sugar contains a small amount of cornstarch, which acts as a binding agent. If you make whipped cream with confectioners' sugar it will not separate as easily as cream beaten with granulated sugar.

Layered Chip and Coconut Bars

I actually developed the recipe for gluten-free graham crackers so that this sinfully rich cookie could be part of this book. A few kinds of candy chips, chewy sweet coconut, and nuts round out the flavors.

Yield: 2 to 3 dozen

Active time: 15 minutes

Start to finish: 1 hour

1 cup coarsely chopped pecans

1 cup crumbs made from Graham Crackers (page 50)

½ cup gluten-free rolled oats

¼ pound (1 stick) unsalted butter, melted and cooled

1 (14-ounce) can sweetened condensed milk

1 cup white chocolate chips

1 cup butterscotch chips

1 cup shredded coconut

1. Preheat the oven to 350°F, and grease a 9 x 9-inch pan. Place pecans on a baking sheet, and toast for 5 to 7 minutes, or until lightly browned.

2. Combine pecans, Graham Cracker crumbs, oats, and butter in a mixing bowl. Mix well. Pat mixture into the prepared pan.

3. Pour sweetened condensed milk over crust, and spread into an even layer. Sprinkle white chocolate and butterscotch chips over milk, and then top with coconut. Press topping down lightly with your fingers or the back of a spoon.

4. Bake for 25 to 30 minutes, or until coconut is brown. Cool completely in the pan on a cooling rack, then cut into pieces.

Variation

✳ *Substitute 1 cup chopped dried fruit or raisins for 1 cup of the chips.*

Born in 1801, Gail Borden, Jr. was the American inventor of condensed milk in 1856, although a similar product had appeared a few years earlier in England. Borden insisted that farmers who wanted to sell him raw milk had to keep their facilities and their cows clean and sanitary. By 1858 Borden's milk, sold as Eagle Brand, had gained a reputation for purity, durability, and economy.

White Chocolate Walnut Blondies

The combination of delicate white chocolate with the crunchy pecans makes these quick and easy brownies more sophisticated than most.

Yield: 2 to 3 dozen
Active time: 15 minutes
Start to finish: 1 hour

1 cup chopped walnuts

⅔ cup brown rice flour

⅓ cup potato starch

½ teaspoon xanthan gum

Pinch of salt

¼ pound (1 stick) unsalted butter, softened

1⅓ cups firmly packed light brown sugar

2 large eggs, at room temperature

1 teaspoon pure vanilla extract

1 cup white chocolate chips

1. Preheat the oven to 350°F and grease an 8 x 8-inch baking pan. Place walnuts on a baking sheet, and toast for 5 to 7 minutes, or until lightly browned.

2. Combine rice flour, potato starch, xanthan gum, and salt in a mixing bowl. Whisk well.

3. Combine butter and brown sugar in another mixing bowl and beat at low speed with an electric mixer to combine. Increase the speed to high, and beat for 3 to 4 minutes, or until light and fluffy.

4. Reduce the mixer speed to medium and beat in the eggs, one at a time, and the vanilla. Reduce the speed to low and add the rice flour mixture. Mix until just blended. Stir in walnuts and white chocolate, and spread the batter to an even layer in the prepared pan.

5. Bake for 40 minutes, or until a toothpick inserted in the center comes out clean. Cool completely in the pan on a cooling rack, then cut into pieces.

Variation
✳ *Substitute bittersweet chocolate chips for the white chocolate, and pecans for the walnuts.*

White chocolate is not officially chocolate, since it doesn't contain the thick, dark paste that remains once the cocoa butter is removed. It has the cocoa butter as its base, along with sugar and milk solids. It has a tendency to clump and should be melted over very low heat to keep it creamy.

Marble Fudge Brownies

I adore the combination of chocolate and cream cheese, and these brownies deliver both. These are always a hit when served, and they can also be frozen for up to a month, so make a double batch.

Yield: 2 to 3 dozen

Active time: 15 minutes

Start to finish: 1 hour

Rice flour

4 ounces semisweet chocolate, chopped

¼ pound (1 stick) unsalted butter

3 large eggs, divided

1 cup granulated sugar, divided

½ cup brown rice flour

¼ teaspoon xanthan gum

Pinch of salt

1 (8-ounce) package cream cheese, softened

½ teaspoon pure vanilla extract

1. Preheat the oven to 350°F. Grease a 9 x 9-inch baking pan, and dust it with rice flour.

2. Melt chocolate and butter in a heavy saucepan over low heat, stirring frequently until the mixture is melted and smooth. Remove the pan from the heat, and set aside for 5 to 7 minutes to cool. This can also be done in a microwave oven.

3. Combine 2 eggs and ¾ cup sugar in mixing bowl. Beat with an electric mixer on medium speed for 1 minute, or until well combined. Add cooled chocolate mixture, and beat for 1 minute. Add rice flour, xanthan gum, and salt and beat at low speed until just blended.

4. In another bowl, combine cream cheese, remaining ¼ cup sugar, remaining 1 egg, and vanilla. Beat with an electric mixer on medium speed for 2 minutes, or until light and fluffy. Spread chocolate batter into the prepared pan. Top with cream cheese batter and swirl layers together with small spatula.

5. Bake for 35 minutes, or until the top is springy to the touch. Cool completely in the pan on a cooling rack, then cut into pieces.

Note: Keep brownies in an airtight container, layered between sheets of waxed paper or parchment, at room temperature for up to 5 days. You can freeze them for up to a month.

Variation

✳ *Add 1 tablespoon instant espresso powder to the chocolate batter for mocha brownies.*

The Aztecs first discovered chocolate, and our word comes from the Aztec *xocolatl*, which means "bitter water." Famed King Montezuma believed chocolate was an aphrodisiac and is reported to have consumed some 50 cups a day.

Fudgy Hazelnut Brownies

I adore the combination of chocolate and hazelnut, and these brownies are like a cookie version of popular Nutella spread. If you want to dress them up for the holidays, try some candied orange peel as a garnish.

Yield: 2 to 3 dozen

Active time: 15 minutes

Start to finish: 1 hour

Rice flour

4 ounces unsweetened chocolate

¼ pound (1 stick) unsalted butter

1 cup skinned hazelnuts

½ teaspoon pure vanilla extract

2 large eggs, at room temperature

1¼ cups granulated sugar

¼ teaspoon xanthan gum

Pinch of salt

⅓ cup brown rice flour

3 tablespoons cornstarch

3 tablespoons unsweetened cocoa powder

½ cup confectioners' sugar for dusting

1. Preheat the oven to 350°F. Grease an 8 x 8-inch baking pan and dust it with rice flour.

2. Melt chocolate and butter in a heavy saucepan over low heat, stirring frequently until the mixture is melted and smooth. Remove the pan from the heat, and set aside for 5 to 7 minutes to cool. This can also be done in a microwave oven.

3. Place hazelnuts on a baking sheet, and toast for 5 to 7 minutes, or until browned, and set aside.

4. Combine vanilla, eggs, sugar, xanthan gum, and salt in a bowl, and whisk well. Stir in the cooled chocolate mixture, and beat well. Add rice flour, cornstarch, and cocoa powder, and mix well. Then stir in hazelnuts. Scrape batter into the prepared pan, and smooth the top.

5. Bake for 45 minutes, or until the top is dry and a toothpick inserted in the center comes out barely clean. Cool completely in the pan on a cooling rack, then cut into pieces. Dust squares with confectioners' sugar.

Variations
* *Substitute whole peanuts, chopped pecans, or walnuts for the hazelnuts.*
* *Add ½ cup miniature chocolate chips to the batter along with the nuts.*

> **Cocoa powder has a tendency to become lumpy if exposed to humidity, and if you find that this is the case with your container, sift the cocoa or shake it through a fine-meshed sieve before using it. Those little lumps are difficult to remove otherwise.**

Chocolate Peppermint Brownies

These brownies with a double dose of chocolate are topped with a creamy peppermint frosting, and then made even prettier with some crushed candies.

Yield: 2 to 3 dozen miniatures

Active time: 15 minutes

Start to finish: 1 hour

3 ounces bittersweet chocolate, chopped

⅓ cup heavy cream, divided

½ cup amaranth flour

½ cup almond meal

3 tablespoons unsweetened cocoa powder

½ teaspoon xanthan gum

½ teaspoon salt

12 tablespoons (1½ sticks) unsalted butter, softened, divided

2½ cups confectioners' sugar, divided

2 large eggs

½ teaspoon pure vanilla extract

½ to 1 teaspoon mint oil

2 to 4 drops red food coloring (optional)

¾ cup crushed red and white peppermint candies

1. Preheat the oven to 350°F, and grease a 9 x 9-inch baking pan. Combine chocolate and 2 tablespoons cream in a microwave safe bowl. Microwave on medium (50 percent power) at 30 second intervals, stirring between intervals, until chocolate is melted and smooth. Set aside.

2. Combine amaranth flour, almond meal, cocoa powder, xanthan gum, and salt in a mixing bowl. Whisk well.

3. Combine 8 tablespoons butter and ½ cup confectioners' sugar in another mixing bowl and beat at low speed with an electric mixer to combine. Increase the speed to high, and beat for 3 to 4 minutes, or until light and fluffy. Add eggs, one at a time, and beat well between each addition. Beat in cooled chocolate and vanilla. Slowly add dry ingredients to the butter mixture, and beat until dough forms.

4. Scrape batter into the prepared pan, and bake for 15 minutes, or until firm and a toothpick inserted into the center comes out clean. Cool completely in the pan on a cooling rack.

5. For frosting, combine remaining butter and remaining sugar in a mixing bowl, and add 2 tablespoons of the remaining cream. Beat at medium speed with an electric mixer until light and fluffy. Add mint oil and red food coloring, if using, and beat well. Add additional cream by 1-teaspoon amounts if frosting is too thick to spread.

6. Spread frosting over brownies, and sprinkle crushed candies evenly over frosting. Cut into pieces.

Variation

* *For chocolate almond brownies, substitute pure almond extract for the mint oil, omit the food coloring, and substitute slivered almonds (toasted in a 350°F oven for 7 to 9 minutes) for the peppermint candies.*

> Because chocolate can absorb aromas and flavors from other foods, it should always be wrapped tightly after being opened. Store chocolate in a cool, dry place, but it should not be refrigerated or frozen. If stored at a high temperature, the fat will rise to the surface and become a whitish powder called a bloom. It will disappear, however, as soon as the chocolate is melted.

Peanut Butter and Chocolate Layered Brownies

These chocolate brownies are topped with a layer of peanut butter frosting, which is then coated with even more chocolate for a sinfully rich and delicious treat.

Yield: 3 to 4 dozen

Active time: 25 minutes

Start to finish: 2 hours

1½ cups (2½ sticks) unsalted butter, softened, divided

3 ounces unsweetened chocolate, chopped

14 ounces bittersweet chocolate, chopped, divided

1½ cups granulated sugar

1½ teaspoons pure vanilla extract, divided

¼ teaspoon salt

4 large eggs

⅔ cup brown rice flour

⅓ cup potato starch

½ teaspoon xanthan gum

1 cup roasted salted peanuts, coarsely chopped

1 cup chunky commercial peanut butter (do not use natural)

¾ cup confectioners' sugar

1 tablespoon whole milk

7 ounces bittersweet chocolate, chopped

1. Preheat the oven to 325°F. Line a 9 x 13-inch baking pan with heavy-duty aluminum foil, allowing the sides to be long and wrapped around the sides of the pan. Grease the foil.

2. Melt ¾ cup (1½ sticks) butter, unsweetened chocolate, and half of the bittersweet chocolate in a heavy saucepan over low heat, stirring frequently. Remove the pan from the heat, and set aside for 5 to 7 minutes to cool. This can also be done in a microwave oven.

3. Whisk granulated sugar, 1 teaspoon vanilla, and salt, then eggs, 1 at a time into cooled chocolate. Whisk in rice flour, potato starch, and xanthan gum. Fold in chopped peanuts. Spread batter evenly in the prepared pan.

4. Bake for 30 minutes, or until a toothpick inserted into the center comes out with moist crumbs attached. Cool completely in the pan on a cooling rack.

5. Combine peanut butter and 4 tablespoons of remaining butter in a mixing bowl, and beat at low speed with an electric mixer to combine. Add confectioners' sugar, milk, and remaining ½ teaspoon vanilla, and beat for 2 minutes, or until light and fluffy. Spread mixture on top of brownies, and chill brownies for 1 hour.

6. Combine remaining chocolate and remaining butter in a small saucepan, and melt over low heat. Stir until smooth. Place dollops of chocolate on top of peanut butter layer, and spread gently to cover peanut butter layer completely.

7. Chill brownies, lightly covered with plastic wrap, for at least 1 hour, or until chocolate is firm.

8. Remove brownies from the pan by pulling up on the sides of the foil. Cut into pieces. Bring to room temperature before serving.

Note: Keep brownies refrigerated in an airtight container, layered between sheets of waxed paper or parchment. They will keep fresh for up to 3 days.

> Peanuts are used in cuisines around the world, but peanut butter is a home-grown American invention. It was developed in 1890 and first promoted as a health food at the 1904 World's Fair in St. Louis.

CHAPTER 6:

Gluten-Free from the Start:
Meringues and Macaroons

Long before we knew about gluten intolerance, many people knew that they could eat crisp meringues and chewy macaroons without negative repercussions. What unites the two is that the base for both is egg whites.

For meringues, the whites are stiffly beaten and strengthened with sugar before the additions are folded in. Macaroons are somewhat different. Classic French macarons (with only one letter "o") are similar to meringues, but also include almond meal. However, our all-American macaroons are a category that includes any myriad cookies bound by egg white—from ground cashews to coconut.

While most American recipes for meringues are rather plain and just involve folding ingredients into the frothy matrix, classic French cooking includes many meringue forms that are fancier and make great additions to Christmas collections. You'll find recipes for both in this chapter.

Eggs Whites 101

The key to all the recipes in this chapter is properly handling the egg whites. Start the process by washing your hands, since any grease on hands that the egg whites touch can harm the meringue. Crack the egg gently in the center on a flat surface such as your counter, and not on the edge of the bowl. Pull apart the two halves, holding them over the bowl. Move the yolk from shell to shell until almost no white remains attached to the yolk.

While separating the eggs, place each white in a separate small bowl, and then transfer to the large bowl of egg whites. This ensures that a bit of yolk does not ruin a whole bowl of egg whites. (The yolk contains fat and will keep the whites from foaming.) If the yolk breaks, place whatever contents remain in the shell into the bowl with the yolks, and do not attempt to extricate more egg white from that particular egg.

Allow the egg whites to stand at room temperature for 30 minutes before beating. This enables the maximum amount of air to be absorbed and will provide the greatest volume. To hasten the process, place the bowl of whites in a larger bowl of warm water for a few minutes, stirring once or twice.

The bowl used for beating must be absolutely clean and dry. Any trace of fat or grease may prevent egg whites from reaching their full volume or even creating foam. It's best to rinse the bowl and beaters with vinegar or lemon to make sure not a trace of fat remains. The best bowl for beating egg whites is a copper bowl, as the copper ions bind to the egg and will stabilize the beaten whites. The next best choice is a stainless steel or glass bowl. Plastic bowls tend to absorb fat from other dishes, even if the bowl has been very well cleaned. Egg whites can also react with metal ions from an aluminum bowl. The ions may form dark particles that can give the beaten egg whites a grayish color.

Start by beating the egg whites at moderately slow speed until they are foaming, about 2 minutes. Gradually increase the speed to fast, and continue until soft peaks form. In most dessert recipes, a few tablespoons of sugar are sprinkled over the meringue, and then beating is continued to form stiff peaks and a glossy surface. Here are some tips for marvelous meringues:

• Adding an acid ingredient will help stabilize the foam of beaten egg whites. Cream of tartar, lemon juice, and salt will help keep the whites smooth and foamy. Add them *after* you have beaten the whites until they are frothy. While the acid does stabilize the foamy whites, it can actually slow down the foaming process. Continue to beat until soft peaks form. Use ⅛ teaspoon of cream of tartar for each 2 to 3 egg whites.

• Do not let your whipped egg whites or foam sit for very long before folding in other ingredients. Within minutes the foam will slowly begin to shrink or separate.

• To salvage over-beaten egg whites, whip in a tablespoon or two of unbeaten egg white.

• Make sure sugar is completely dissolved in the beating process or the meringue will be gritty.

Note: Unless otherwise noted in the recipe, store these cookies by keeping them in an airtight container, layered between sheets of waxed paper or parchment, at room temperature for up to 5 days.

Fancy French Macarons

The title of this recipe is not a typo; in French it's macarons *with only one "o." And oh, are these famed cookies a treat! The chewy cookies can be flavored in myriad ways, and filled with anything from chocolate ganache to raspberry jam.*

Yield: 3 dozen

Active time: 25 minutes

Start to finish: 1 hour

2¾ cup confectioners' sugar

2¼ cups almond meal

7 large egg whites, at room temperature

½ teaspoon cream of tartar

¼ teaspoon salt

¾ cup superfine granulated sugar

4 to 6 drops food coloring (optional)

½ cup Buttercream Icing (page 24)

¼ teaspoon pure extract or oil (such as vanilla, almond, lemon, orange, raspberry, or rum)

1. Preheat the oven to 300°F. Line two baking sheets with parchment paper or silicon baking mats.

2. Combine confectioners' sugar and almond meal in a food processor fitted with the steel blade and process until smooth. Shake mixture through a fine sieve into a mixing bowl. Use bits of almond remaining in the strainer for another recipe.

3. Place egg whites in a grease-free mixing bowl and beat at medium speed with an electric mixer until frothy. Add the cream of tartar and salt, raise the speed to high, and beat until soft peaks form. Add sugar, 1 tablespoon at a time, and continue to beat until stiff peaks form and meringue is glossy. Beat in food coloring, if using.

4. Fold meringue into almond sugar mixture. Fill a pastry bag fitted with a ½-inch plain tip with meringue. Pipe out 2½-inch circles, spacing them 1 inch apart. Tap the baking sheet on the counter and allow meringues to sit for 10 minutes.

5. Bake meringues for 13 to 15 minutes or until tops are dry. Allow macarons to cool completely on the baking sheets on top of a wire rack, then transfer to the cooling rack.

6. Bring Buttercream Icing to room temperature, and stir in extract. Spread 1 heaping teaspoon Buttercream Icing on flat side of one cookie, and sandwich with a second cookie.

Note: Keep cookies in an airtight container, refrigerated, layered between sheets of waxed paper or parchment for up to 3 days.

Variations
* *Melt 1 tablespoon instant espresso powder in 1 tablespoon boiling water. Let it cool and beat it into meringue instead of food coloring.*
* *Substitute thick fruit jam for the buttercream icing.*

> **Macaroons are among the oldest cookies around. Records show that chefs in the royal court were making them as early as the mid-sixteenth century. Our English word macaroon comes from the French *macarons*, which comes from the Italian word *maccarone*, which means a small cake made with almonds. It's likely that Catherine de Medici brought them to France from Italy when she arrived in 1533.**

Double Chocolate French Macarons

These pretty, light brown cookies are filled with rich and dense chocolate ganache for a contrast of textures as well as intensity of chocolate flavors.

Yield: 2 dozen

Active time: 25 minutes

Start to finish: 1 hour

1½ cups confectioners' sugar

¾ cup almond meal

⅓ cup unsweetened cocoa powder

3 large egg whites, at room temperature

¼ teaspoon cream of tartar

Pinch of salt

½ cup superfine granulated sugar

4 to 6 drops food coloring (optional)

½ cup heavy cream

1 tablespoon light corn syrup

5 ounces bittersweet chocolate, chopped

1. Preheat the oven to 300°F. Line two baking sheets with parchment paper or silicon baking mats.

2. Combine confectioners' sugar, almond meal, and cocoa in a food processor fitted with the steel blade and process until smooth. Shake mixture through a fine sieve into a mixing bowl. Use bits of almond remaining in the strainer for another use.

3. Place egg whites in a grease-free mixing bowl and beat at medium speed with an electric mixer until frothy. Add the cream of tartar and salt, raise the speed to high, and beat until soft peaks form. Add sugar, 1 tablespoon at a time, and continue to beat until stiff peaks form and meringue is glossy. Beat in food coloring, if using.

4. Fold meringue into almond cocoa mixture. Fill a pastry bag fitted with a ½-inch plain tip with meringue. Pipe out 2-inch circles, spacing them 1 inch apart. Tap the baking sheet on the counter and allow meringues to sit for 10 minutes.

5. Bake meringues for 13 to 15 minutes or until tops are dry. Allow macarons to cool completely on the baking sheets on top of a wire rack, then transfer to the cooling rack.

6. While meringues cool, prepare chocolate. Combine cream and corn syrup in a small saucepan, and stir over medium heat until cream begins to simmer. Remove the pan from the heat, and stir in chocolate. Stir until chocolate is melted. Let cool until thickened before using.

7. Spread 1 heaping teaspoon chocolate on the flat side of one cookie, and sandwich with a second cookie.

Note: Keep cookies in an airtight container, refrigerated, layered between sheets of waxed paper or parchment for up to 3 days.

Variations
* *Add ½ teaspoon rum or orange extract to chocolate filling.*
* *Substitute white chocolate for bittersweet chocolate in the filling.*

> **To fill a pastry bag:** Place the tip into the bag, and then use a few heavy paper clips to shut the bag above the top of the tip. Place the pastry bag in a beaker with the top tucked over the sides, and then fill it. Remove the bag from the beaker, remove the paper clips, and use the clips to keep the top firmly closed as you pipe.

Almond Pine Nut Macaroons

I was thrilled to discover that almond paste, made from ground almonds, was gluten-free. These macaroons are very quick and easy to make, and topping them with pine nuts is the way they're served in Italy.

Yield: 3 dozen

Active time: 15 minutes

Start to finish: 40 minutes

1 (8-ounce) can
almond paste

1¼ cups granulated sugar

2 large egg whites,
at room temperature

¾ cup pine nuts

1. Preheat the oven to 325°F, and line two baking sheets with parchment paper or silicon baking mats.

2. Break almond paste into small pieces and place it in a mixing bowl along with sugar. Beat at medium speed with an electric mixer until combined. Increase the speed to high, add egg whites, and beat until mixture is light and fluffy. This can also be done in a food processor fitted with the steel blade.

3. Drop heaping tablespoons of dough onto the prepared baking sheets. Pat pine nuts into tops of cookies.

4. Bake cookies for 18 to 20 minutes, or until lightly browned. Place baking sheets on wire racks, and cool completely.

Variation
✻ *Substitute chopped blanched almonds or chopped walnuts for the pine nuts.*

> **Make sure when buying the almond paste that it's almond paste and not marzipan, which is already sweetened.**

Coconut Macaroons

Coconut macaroons are always chewy; that's what happens when coconut is melded with egg whites. But these are very special because the coconut is toasted first.

Yield: 3 dozen

Active time: 15 minutes

Start to finish: 45 minutes

4 cups unsweetened shredded coconut

5 large egg whites, at room temperature

½ teaspoon cream of tartar

¼ teaspoon salt

1½ cups superfine granulated sugar

1 teaspoon pure vanilla extract

1. Preheat the oven to 350°F, and line two baking sheets with parchment paper or silicon baking mats. Place coconut on a baking sheet, and toast for 7 to 10 minutes, or until lightly browned. Set aside to cool. Reduce the oven temperature to 275°F.

2. Place egg whites in a grease-free mixing bowl and beat at medium speed with an electric mixer until frothy. Add the cream of tartar and salt, raise the speed to high, and beat until soft peaks form. Add sugar, 1 tablespoon at a time, and continue to beat until stiff peaks form and meringue is glossy. Beat in vanilla. Fold cooled coconut into meringue.

3. Drop meringue by heaping 1-tablespoon portions onto prepared baking sheets, 1½ inches apart. Bake for 25 to 30 minutes, or until outside of macaroons are dry. Cool cookies on the baking sheets on top of cooling racks.

Variation
* *Substitute ½ cup toasted chopped almonds for ½ cup of the coconut, and substitute pure almond extract for the vanilla.*

You can find unsweetened coconut in health food stores and the bulk bin areas of many supermarkets. If you can't find it and end up using sweetened baking coconut, cut back on the sugar to 1 cup, and only toast the coconut for 3 to 5 minutes.

101

Cashew Macaroons

Cashews are a nut often overlooked when baking cookies, and these nutty macaroons will make you a convert.

Yield: 3 dozen

Active time: 15 minutes

Start to finish: 30 minutes

2 cups raw cashews

1¼ cups granulated sugar

2 large egg whites,
at room temperature

Pinch of salt

½ teaspoon pure
vanilla extract

Gluten-free sugar sprinkles

36 cashews for garnish

1. Preheat the oven to 350°F. Line two baking sheets with parchment paper or silicon baking mats.

2. Combine cashews and sugar in a food processor fitted with the steel blade. Process until nuts are finely ground. Add egg whites, salt, and vanilla to the food processor, and process until well combined.

3. Form dough into 1-inch balls, and roll them in sugar sprinkles. Arrange cookies on the baking sheets, and press a cashew in the center of each.

4. Bake cookies for 10 to 12 minutes, or until lightly brown. Cool cookies for 2 minutes on the baking sheets, and then transfer them with a spatula to cooling racks to cool completely.

Variation

✳ *Substitute blanched almonds for the cashews, and almond extract for the vanilla extract.*

Egg white is very high in protein, with almost no fat, and virtually no cholesterol. It has merely 13 percent of the calories of a whole egg, and the other nutrient in egg whites is B-2 or riboflavin.

Cocoa Chocolate Chip Meringues

Unsweetened cocoa powder is a great addition to crispy meringue cookies, and miniature chocolate chips give the chocolate flavor a further boost.

Yield: 3 dozen

Active time: 20 minutes

Start to finish: 1½ hours

3 large egg whites, at room temperature

¼ teaspoon cream of tartar

Pinch of salt

¾ cup superfine granulated sugar

⅓ cup unsweetened cocoa powder

½ teaspoon pure vanilla extract

1 cup miniature chocolate chips

1. Preheat the oven to 275°F. Line two baking sheets with parchment paper or silicon baking mats.

2. Place egg whites in a grease-free mixing bowl and beat at medium speed with an electric mixer until frothy. Add the cream of tartar and salt, raise the speed to high, and beat until soft peaks form. Add sugar, 1 tablespoon at a time, and continue to beat until stiff peaks form and meringue is glossy. Beat in cocoa and vanilla. Fold chocolate chips into meringue.

3. Pipe meringues with a pastry bag fitted with a large star tip by heaping 1-tablespoon portions onto prepared baking sheets. Bake for 30 minutes. Turn off the oven, and allow meringues to stay in the oven for an additional 30 minutes. Transfer to a cooling rack to cool completely.

Variations

* *Substitute pure almond extract, mint oil, or mint extract for the vanilla.*

* *Substitute 1 cup chopped pecans or walnuts, toasted in a 350ºF oven for 5 to 7 minutes, for the chocolate chips.*

> If you want crisp meringues, serve them on the same day they're made; they soften even when stored in an airtight container. They also soften very quickly in a humid environment.

Praline Meringues

Using brown sugar rather than white sugar creates a really special flavor for these cookies. They're as rich as a praline candy, but the texture is much lighter.

Yield: 3 dozen

Active time: 20 minutes

Start to finish: 1½ hours

2 cups chopped pecans

5 large egg whites, at room temperature

⅓ teaspoon cream of tartar

¼ teaspoon salt

1½ cups firmly packed dark brown sugar

½ teaspoon pure vanilla extract

1. Preheat the oven to 275°F. Line two baking sheets with parchment paper or silicon baking mats. Place pecans on a baking sheet, and toast for 5 to 7 minutes, or until lightly browned. Set aside.

2. Place egg whites in a grease-free mixing bowl and beat at medium speed with an electric mixer until frothy. Add the cream of tartar and salt, raise the speed to high, and beat until soft peaks form. Add brown sugar, 1 tablespoon at a time, and continue to beat until stiff peaks form and meringue is glossy. Beat in vanilla. Fold cooled nuts into meringue.

3. Pipe meringues with a pastry bag fitted with a large star tip by heaping 1-tablespoon portions onto prepared baking sheets. Bake for 30 minutes. Turn off the oven, and allow meringues to stay in the oven for an additional 30 minutes. Transfer to a cooling rack to cool completely.

Variations
✳ *Substitute almonds or peanuts for the pecans.*
✳ *Substitute ½ teaspoon apple pie spice for the vanilla.*

> **It is possible to overbeat the whites. When overbeaten, the whites tend to form clumps, which do not blend easily with other ingredients. Whipped egg whites should expand with heat, but if they are beaten until too stiff, they will be inelastic and will not expand when heated.**

CHAPTER 7:

Candy Is Dandy:
Unbaked Gluten-Free Confections

All categories of candy—from red-and-white striped peppermint canes to seductive and luscious chocolate truffles—are part of most collections of Christmas treats. But for those who are gluten-intolerant, these candies are usually off limits if commercially made; the factory could easily be making cookies with wheat flour, which is usually enough to cause contamination.

The recipes in this chapter are all open to personal interpretation, another reason for making treats in your own kitchen. They include decadently rich chocolate truffles, different types of fudge, and variations on nougat—another classic holiday treat.

The best way to include candies as part of your holiday treat collection is to put the morsels into small paper cups, and do keep the pieces small! They're very rich, and a one-inch cube is about the right size.

Sugar Stages

Most candy recipes instruct you to boil your sugar mixture until it reaches a certain temperature. The final texture of candy depends on the sugar concentration. As the syrup is heated, it boils, water evaporates, the sugar concentration increases, and the boiling point rises. A given temperature corresponds to a particular sugar concentration. In general, higher temperatures and greater sugar concentrations result in hard, brittle candies, and lower temperatures result in softer candies.

For the best results and most accuracy, use a candy thermometer. However, if you don't have one, there is a classic test conducted by dropping a few droplets of the boiling syrup into ice water and then feeling the result. If you want to practice this, bring some sugar syrup to a boil, and then test it every few minutes to feel the result. Here are the stages of sugar:

- **Thread stage:** 230 to 233°F, with sugar concentration at 80 percent. This is used for the sorts of syrup you'd use on ice cream. At this temperature the liquid forms threads, but does not form a ball.

- **Soft ball stage:** 234 to 240°F, with sugar concentration at 85 percent. This is the temperature used for fudge and other soft candies. Sugar syrup dropped into cold water will form a soft, flexible ball. If you remove the ball from water, it will flatten like a pancake after a few moments in your hand.

- **Firm ball stage:** 244 to 248°F, with sugar concentration at 87 percent. This is the temperature used for caramel candies and other candies with medium density. Drop a little of this syrup in cold water and it will form a firm ball, one that won't flatten when you take it out of the water, but remains malleable and will flatten when squeezed.

- **Hard ball stage:** 250 to 266°F, with sugar concentration at 92 percent. This is the temperature for nougat and other chewy and dense candy. A little of this syrup dropped into cold water will form a hard ball. If you take the ball out of the water, it won't flatten. The ball will be hard, but you can still change its shape by squashing it.

- **Soft crack stage:** 270 to 290°F, with sugar concentration at 95 percent. Saltwater taffy is made with sugar at this temperature. As the syrup reaches soft-crack stage, the bubbles on top will become smaller, thicker, and closer together. At this stage, the moisture content is low. When you drop a bit of this syrup into cold water, it will solidify into threads that, when removed from the water, are flexible, not brittle. They will bend slightly before breaking.

- **Hard crack stage:** 295 to 310°F with a sugar concentration of 99 percent. This temperature is needed for brittles and butter toffee. The hard-crack stage is the highest temperature you are likely to see specified in a candy recipe. At these temperatures, there is almost no water left in the syrup. Drop a little of the molten syrup in cold water and it will form hard, brittle threads that break when bent.

- **Caramelized sugar:** 320 to 340°F, with a sugar concentration of 100 percent. At the lower end of this range the liquid is clear, and as it climbs in temperature, it turns to a golden and then deeper brown. This is what is used to make caramel sauce, not caramel candies.

Note: The temperatures specified here are for sea level. At higher altitudes, subtract 1°F from every listed temperature for each 500 feet above sea level.

As you can see, a few degrees in one direction or another can change the results of the candy, so it's a good idea to test your thermometer's accuracy by placing it in plain boiling water. At sea level, it should read 212°F. If it reads above or below this number, make the necessary adjustments when cooking your sugar syrup.

Chocolate Walnut Fudge

This recipe is Nirvana for all of us who are admitted chocoholics! There's depth from unsweetened chocolate and intensity from bittersweet. Plus crunchy nuts.

Yield: 81 pieces

Active time: 25 minutes

Start to finish: 1¾ hours

1 cup coarsely chopped walnuts

¾ pound (12 ounces) good-quality bittersweet chocolate

2 ounces unsweetened chocolate

¼ pound (1 stick) unsalted butter, sliced

2 cups granulated sugar

1 cup evaporated milk

1 teaspoon pure vanilla extract

Vegetable oil spray

1. Preheat the oven to 350°F. Line a 9 x 9-inch baking pan with heavy-duty aluminum foil, allowing it to extend over the top of the sides. Spray the foil with vegetable oil spray.

2. Place walnuts on a baking sheet, and toast for 5 to 7 minutes, or until lightly browned. Remove nuts from the oven, and set aside.

3. Break bittersweet chocolate and unsweetened chocolate into pieces no larger than a lima bean. Either chop chocolate in a food processor fitted with a steel blade using on-and-off pulsing, or place it in a heavy re-sealable plastic bag, and smash it with the back of a heavy skillet. Place chocolate and butter in a mixing bowl, and set aside.

4. Combine sugar and evaporated milk in a deep saucepan, and cook over medium heat until sugar dissolves and mixture comes to boil. Continue to cook, stirring constantly, for 15 to 18 minutes, or until mixture registers 236°F on candy thermometer, the soft ball stage.

5. Pour hot mixture over chocolate and butter, and whisk until smooth. Stir in walnuts and vanilla.

6. Spread fudge evenly in the prepared pan. Refrigerate, uncovered, for 1 to 2 hours, or until cold and set. Lift fudge from the pan with the foil, and cut into squares.

Note: The squares can be stored refrigerated for up to 1 week. Place them in an airtight container with sheets of plastic wrap in between the layers.

Variations
* *Add 1 tablespoon instant espresso powder to the milk for mocha fudge.*
* *Substitute pure orange extract for the vanilla, and substitute ½ cup chopped candied orange peel and ½ cup dried cranberries.*

Vassar College, one of the Seven Sister schools, is the birthplace of fudge. In 1886, Emelyn Hartridge, a Vassar student, reported that this thick confection was being sold in Baltimore for the astronomical sum of 40 cents a pound, so she made thirty pounds of it to raise money for the Vassar Senior Auction. From there its fame spread to other women's colleges such as Mt. Holyoke and Smith, and then into actual cookbooks.

Southern Pecan Pralines

Pralines are part of the tradition of Southern sweets, and these are incredibly easy to make. The cream and butter balance the sweetness with richness, too.

Yield: 3 dozen

Active time: 25 minutes

Start to finish: 1 hour

3 cups pecan halves

3 cups firmly packed light brown sugar

1 cup heavy cream

½ teaspoon cream of tartar

½ teaspoon salt

4 tablespoons (½ stick) unsalted butter, thinly sliced

¾ teaspoon pure vanilla extract

Vegetable oil spray

1. Preheat the oven to 350°F. Place pecans on a baking sheet, and toast for 5 to 7 minutes, or until lightly browned. Spray two baking sheets with vegetable oil spray.

2. Combine brown sugar, cream, cream of tartar, and salt in a saucepan. Place the pan over medium heat, and swirl the pan by its handle until sugar dissolves. Raise the heat to medium-high, and continue to cook, stirring constantly, for 15 to 18 minutes, or until mixture registers 236°F on a candy thermometer, the soft ball stage.

3. Stir in butter and vanilla, and cool mixture to a temperature of 220°F. Beat at medium speed with an electric mixer for 2 minutes, or until mixture is creamy. Stir in pecans.

4. Drop mixture by 1-tablespoon portions onto the prepared baking sheets. Let pralines harden at room temperature.

Note: The pralines can be stored at room temperature for up to 1 week. Place them in an airtight container with sheets of waxed paper in between the layers.

Variation
✳ *For New England Pralines, substitute walnut halves for the pecans, and substitute maple sugar for the light brown sugar.*

It is widely agreed that pralines are named after a French diplomat from the early seventeenth century whose name and title was César, duc de Choiseul, comte du Plessis-Praslin. The actual creator of the praline is believed to be his personal chef, Clement Lassagne, but there are many versions of the story.

Peanut Penuche

Penuche (pronounced pan-OU-see*) is an old-fashioned candy made with brown sugar and butter. It's most popular on the Eastern Seaboard, where it contains anything from a variety of nuts to marshmallow cream. It's a great addition to a Christmas selection, especially for people allergic to chocolate.*

Yield: 64 pieces

Active time: 15 minutes

Start to finish: 1½ hours, including 45 minutes to chill

⅔ cup evaporated milk

2 cups firmly packed light brown sugar

12 tablespoons (1½ sticks) unsalted butter, sliced

Pinch of salt

¾ teaspoon pure vanilla extract

⅛ teaspoon ground cinnamon

1⅔ cups confectioners' sugar

1 cup roasted peanuts (not dry-roasted)

Vegetable oil spray

1. Line an 8 x 8-inch baking pan with heavy-duty aluminum foil, allowing it to extend over the top of the sides. Spray the foil with vegetable oil spray.

2. Combine evaporated milk, brown sugar, butter, salt, vanilla, and cinnamon in a heavy saucepan, and whisk well. Bring to a boil over medium heat, stirring until sugar dissolves.

3. Reduce the heat to low and simmer, stirring frequently, for 25 to 30 minutes or until mixture registers 238°F on candy thermometer, the soft ball stage.

4. Add confectioners' sugar, ¼ cup at a time, at medium speed with an electric mixer. Beat for 3 to 4 minutes, or until fudge is thick and smooth. Stir in peanuts.

5. Spread fudge evenly in the prepared pan, and refrigerate, uncovered, for 45 minutes, or until firm enough to cut. Remove fudge from the pan by pulling up on the sides of the foil, and discard the foil. Cut fudge into 1-inch squares with a sharp paring knife.

Note: The squares can be stored refrigerated for up to 1 week. Place them in an airtight container with sheets of plastic wrap in between the layers.

Variations
* *Substitute chopped toasted pecans or walnuts for the peanuts.*
* *Substitute pure almond extract for the vanilla, and omit the cinnamon.*

Believe it or not, there's actually a National Penuche Day. It's celebrated on July 22, although it is unclear how this occurred.

Hazelnut Nougat

This is the traditional way nougat is made in Italy, where it's enjoyed all year long. The aroma of hazelnuts along with the flavor from its liqueur is totally tantalizing.

Yield: 64 pieces

Active time: 30 minutes

Start to finish: 2 hours

⅓ pound skinned hazelnuts

2 large egg whites,
at room temperature

¼ teaspoon cream of tartar

¼ teaspoon salt

1 cup granulated sugar

1 cup honey

1½ cups light corn syrup

¼ cup water

3 tablespoons Frangelico,
or other hazelnut-flavored
liqueur

Vegetable oil spray

Skinning hazelnuts is not a fun task, so try to find them already skinned. If you have to do it yourself, bake them for 25 minutes, then place them in a towel and rub them back and forth. The skins will come off.

1. Preheat the oven to 350°F. Line an 8 x 8-inch square pan with heavy-duty aluminum foil, allowing it to extend over the top of the sides. Spray the foil with vegetable oil spray. Place hazelnuts on a baking sheet, and toast for 5 to 7 minutes, or until lightly browned. Set aside.

2. Place egg whites in a grease-free mixing bowl and beat at medium speed with an electric mixer until frothy. Add the cream of tartar and salt, raise the speed to high, and beat until stiff peaks form.

3. While whites are beating, combine sugar, honey, corn syrup, and water in a saucepan over medium-high heat. Stir until sugar dissolves, and continue to cook until the mixture for 10 to 12 minutes, or until mixture reaches 250°F on a candy thermometer, the hard ball stage.

4. Remove the pan from the heat, and slowly pour approximately ¼ of syrup into egg whites, with the mixer running constantly. Continue to beat egg whites until the mixture holds its shape.

5. Return the saucepan to the stove, and continue to cook over medium-high heat until the mixture reaches 300°F on a candy thermometer, the hard crack stage.

6. With the mixer running, pour remaining sugar syrup slowly into egg mixture and continue beating until mixture is thick and stiff. Add Frangelico and hazelnuts, and beat just until combined.

7. Spoon nougat into the prepared pan, and press it smoothly and evenly. Place a sheet of parchment paper on top, and weight it with another 8 x 8-inch baking pan filled with cans. Refrigerate nougat until cold and set. Remove nougat from the pan using the foil as a guide, and cut into 1-inch squares.

Note: The squares can be stored refrigerated for up to 1 week. Place them in an airtight container with sheets of plastic wrap in between the layers.

Variation
✳ *Substitute chopped toasted almonds for the hazelnuts and amaretto for the Frangelico.*

Spiced Buttery Peanut Brittle

The addition of some aromatic spices from Chinese five-spice powder adds interest to the sweet and crunchy morsels of this typical Southern sweet.

Yield: 3 to 4 dozen pieces

Active time: 25 minutes

Start to finish: 1 hour

½ pound (2 sticks) unsalted butter

1 cup granulated sugar

2 tablespoons water

2 tablespoons light corn syrup

1 teaspoon Chinese five-spice powder

¼ teaspoon salt

1½ cups roasted peanuts (not dry-roasted)

Vegetable oil spray

1. Prepare a lipped baking sheet by lining it with heavy-duty aluminum foil and spraying the foil with vegetable oil spray. Set aside.

2. Melt butter in a medium saucepan over medium heat. Stir in sugar, water, and corn syrup, and mix well. Cook mixture over medium heat, stirring frequently, until it registers 290°F on a candy thermometer, the soft crack stage. Stir in Chinese five-spice powder, salt, and peanuts.

3. Pour mixture immediately onto the prepared baking sheet. Tilt the sheet several times to spread candy in a thin layer. Allow brittle to sit at room temperature until it is completely cool. Break brittle into small pieces.

Note: The brittle can be stored at room temperature for up to 1 week. Place pieces in an airtight container with sheets of waxed paper in between the layers.

Variations

✳ *Substitute any nut for the peanuts. If the nuts are raw, toast them in a 350°F oven for 5 to 7 minutes, or until browned.*

✳ *Substitute cinnamon or apple pie spice for the Chinese five-spice powder.*

> The first notable increase in peanut consumption in the U.S. was in 1860 with the outbreak of the Civil War. Soldiers on both sides turned to peanuts for food. They took their taste for peanuts home with them and peanuts were sold freshly roasted by street vendors and at baseball games and circuses.

Classic Chocolate Truffles

Once you learn how easy it is to produce those rich, dense chocolate truffles that cost a fortune in stores you'll never buy them again. And another benefit is that you can make them in whatever flavors you like.

Yield: 3 dozen

Active time: 20 minutes

Start to finish: 4½ hours, including 4 hours to chill

1 pound good-quality bittersweet chocolate

1¼ cups heavy cream

Pinch of salt

½ cup unsweetened cocoa powder

1. Break chocolate into pieces no larger than a lima bean. Either chop chocolate in a food processor fitted with a steel blade using on-and-off pulsing, or place it in a heavy re-sealable plastic bag, and smash it with the back of a heavy skillet.

2. Heat cream in a saucepan over medium heat, stirring frequently, until mixture comes to a simmer. Stir in salt, and add chocolate. Remove the pan from the heat, cover the pan, and allow chocolate to melt for 5 minutes. Whisk mixture until smooth, and transfer to a 9 x 9-inch baking pan. Chill mixture for at least 4 hours, or overnight.

3. Place cocoa powder in a shallow bowl. Using the large side of a melon baller, scoop out 2 teaspoons of the mixture, and gently form it into a ball. Roll balls in cocoa, and then refrigerate for 30 minutes to set cocoa.

Note: The truffles can be made up to 1 week in advance, and refrigerated, tightly covered with plastic wrap or in an airtight container. Allow them to sit at room temperature for 1 hour before serving.

Variations

✳ *Coat the truffles in toasted coconut, finely chopped nuts, or coarse sugar (either white or colored).*

✳ *Add 2 to 4 tablespoons liquor or liqueur to the truffle mix.*

✳ *Add 1 to 2 tablespoons instant coffee powder or instant espresso powder to make mocha truffles.*

✳ *Add 1 tablespoon grated orange zest to the mixture.*

✳ *Form truffles around a small nut, such as a hazelnut or a peanut.*

✳ *Coat the truffles in dark chocolate or white chocolate or some combination of the two. To do this, melt chopped chocolate in a mixing bowl set over simmering water, or place chopped chocolate in a microwave safe bowl and microwave on high (100 percent power) for 20 seconds, stir, and repeat as necessary until chocolate is smooth and melted. Place a small amount of melted chocolate in the palm of your hand, and roll formed balls in the chocolate.*

> **You're much more hot-blooded than a bowl of truffle filling. Keep a bowl of ice water and a roll of paper towels handy while rolling the truffles. Submerge your hands in the water until they are very cold. Then dry them and roll some truffles, repeating the dunking as necessary.**

White Chocolate Almond Truffles

Delicate almonds and creamy white chocolate are a winning combination in these easy-to-make truffles. Natural almond butter can be found in both whole foods markets and health food stores.

Yield: 2½ dozen

Active time: 20 minutes

Start to finish: 4½ hours, including 4 hours to chill

1 pound good-quality white chocolate

1 cup whipping cream

1 cup natural almond butter

½ cup granulated sugar

Pinch of salt

1 cup blanched almonds

1. Break chocolate into pieces no larger than a lima bean. Either chop chocolate in a food processor fitted with a steel blade using on-and-off pulsing, or place it in a heavy re-sealable plastic bag, and smash it with the back of a heavy skillet.

2. Heat cream, almond butter, sugar, and salt in a saucepan over medium heat, stirring frequently, until mixture comes to a simmer. Stir in chocolate. Remove the pan from the heat, cover the pan, and allow chocolate to melt for 5 minutes. Whisk mixture until smooth, and transfer to a 9 x 9-inch baking pan. Chill mixture for at least 4 hours, or overnight.

3. While mixture chills, preheat the oven to 350°F. Place almonds on a baking sheet, and toast for 5 to 7 minutes, or until lightly browned. Remove the pan from the oven, and finely chop almonds in a food processor fitted with a steel blade, using on-and-off pulsing, or by hand. Set aside.

4. Place chopped almonds in a shallow bowl. Using the large side of a melon baller, scoop out 2 teaspoons mixture, and gently form it into a ball. Roll balls in chopped almonds, and then refrigerate for 30 minutes or until firm.

Note: The truffles can be made up to 1 week in advance, and refrigerated, tightly covered with plastic wrap or in an airtight container. Allow them to sit at room temperature for 1 hour before serving.

Variations
* *Substitute dark chocolate or milk chocolate for the white chocolate.*
* *Coat the truffles in melted chocolate instead of with nuts.*
* *For peanut truffles, substitute natural peanut butter and chopped peanuts, or you can use commercial peanut butter and omit the sugar from the recipe.*
* *Wrap the truffle filling around a nut.*

> We classify almonds as a nut, but that is not true according to their botanical definition. Almonds are botanically a drupe, and are related to peaches, prunes, mangoes, and cherries. A drupe is a type of fruit that has soft flesh around a hard pit that contains a seed. In this case, the seed is the actual almond.

Crispy Peanut Butter Balls

The component parts of the granola you choose to make these healthful snack balls change the nature of the mixture. My favorite contains nuts as well as dried cranberries, but use whatever suits your fancy or whatever you have in the house.

Yield: 3 dozen

Active time: 10 minutes

Start to finish: 40 minutes, including 30 minutes to chill

2 cups gluten-free granola cereal

½ cup commercial peanut butter

3 tablespoons honey

2 to 4 tablespoons freshly squeezed orange juice

1 tablespoon grated orange zest

Vegetable oil spray

1. Finely chop granola in a food processor fitted with the steel blade, using on-and-off pulsing. Set aside.

2. Whisk peanut butter and honey in mixing bowl until smooth. Add granola, orange juice, and orange zest, and stir with a strong spatula until mixed well. Add additional orange juice, if necessary, so mixture stays together.

3. Spray your hands with vegetable oil spray. Make mixture into 1-inch balls, and arrange balls on a baking sheet. Refrigerate for a minimum of 30 minutes.

Note: The balls can be stored refrigerated for up to 1 week. Place them in an airtight container with sheets of plastic wrap in between the layers.

Variations
* *Substitute whole milk for the orange juice, omit the orange zest, and add ½ teaspoon ground cinnamon to the peanut butter and honey mixture before adding the cereal.*
* *Substitute almond butter for the peanut butter. If using natural almond butter, add ½ cup confectioners' sugar.*
* *Add ¾ cup chopped dried fruit.*
* *Add ¾ cup miniature chocolate chips or butterscotch chips.*

> When cooking, the level of seasoning or sweetening of the component ingredients needs to be taken into consideration. In the case of this candy, both the granola and commercial peanut butter have a fair amount of sugar, so the additional honey is more of a binder than a sweetener.

Dried Fruit Coconut Balls

With all the healthful dried fruit and nuts in these confections they can be eaten without much guilt. The combination of fruits along with the sweet honey is really delicious.

Yield: 2½ dozen

Active time: 25 minutes

Start to finish: 55 minutes, including 30 minutes to chill

1 cup cashews

1½ cups shredded sweetened coconut

½ cup finely chopped dried apricots

½ cup dried currants

½ cup finely chopped dried dates

½ cup crumbs from Graham Crackers (page 50)

⅓ cup honey

Vegetable oil spray

1. Preheat the oven to 350°F. Place cashews on a baking sheet, and toast for 5 to 7 minutes, or until lightly browned. Remove the pan from the oven, and finely chop nuts in a food processor fitted with a steel blade, using on-and-off pulsing, or by hand. Set aside. Place coconut on another baking pan, and toast for 10 to 12 minutes, or until browned. Remove the pan from the oven, and set aside.

2. Combine cashews, ½ cup coconut, dried apricots, dried currants, chopped dates, Graham Cracker crumbs, and honey in a mixing bowl. Stir with a strong spatula until mixed well. Add additional honey, if necessary, so mixture stays together.

3. Spray your hands with vegetable oil spray, and place remaining coconut in a shallow bowl. Make mixture into 1½-inch balls, roll balls in coconut, and arrange balls on a baking sheet. Refrigerate for a minimum of 30 minutes.

Note: The balls can be stored refrigerated for up to 1 week. Place them in an airtight container with sheets of plastic wrap between the layers.

Variations
* *Use any combination of dried fruits, and you can also add some shredded sweetened coconut.*
* *Use any nut you like.*
* *Substitute gluten-free crushed ginger snaps for the graham cracker crumbs.*

While all the confections in this chapter are unbaked, many of them call for toasting nuts in the oven. The alternative method is to toast them in a dry skillet set over medium heat, stirring them often.

Dried Fruit Nougat

While I've never been a fan of fruitcake, I adore candied citrus peels and other candied fruits when they're imbedded in this orange-scented candy.

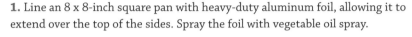

Yield: 64 pieces

Active time: 25 minutes

Start to finish: 2 hours

2 large egg whites,
at room temperature

¼ teaspoon cream of tartar

¼ teaspoon salt

2 cups granulated sugar

1½ cups light corn syrup

¼ cup water

1 tablespoon grated
orange zest

½ teaspoon orange oil or
pure orange extract

1 cup mixed dried fruit
and candied citrus peels,
chopped

Vegetable oil spray

1. Line an 8 x 8-inch square pan with heavy-duty aluminum foil, allowing it to extend over the top of the sides. Spray the foil with vegetable oil spray.

2. Place egg whites in a grease-free mixing bowl and beat at medium speed with an electric mixer until frothy. Add the cream of tartar and salt, raise the speed to high, and beat until stiff peaks form.

3. While whites are beating, combine sugar, corn syrup, and water in a saucepan over medium-high heat. Stir until sugar dissolves, and continue to cook the mixture for 10 to 12 minutes, or until mixture reaches 250°F on a candy thermometer, the hard ball stage.

4. Remove the pan from the heat, and slowly pour approximately ¼ of syrup into egg whites, with the mixer running constantly. Continue to beat egg whites until the mixture holds its shape.

5. Return the saucepan to the stove, and continue to cook over medium-high heat until the mixture reaches 300°F on a candy thermometer, the hard crack stage.

6. With the mixer running, pour remaining sugar syrup slowly into egg mixture and continue beating until mixture is thick and stiff. Add orange zest, orange oil, and dried fruit, and beat just until combined.

7. Spoon nougat into the prepared pan, and press it smoothly and evenly. Place a sheet of parchment paper on top, and weight it with another 8 x 8-inch baking pan filled with cans. Refrigerate nougat until cold and set. Remove nougat from the pan using the foil as a guide, and cut into 1-inch squares.

Note: The squares can be stored refrigerated for up to 1 week. Place them in an airtight container with sheets of plastic wrap in between the layers.

Variation

✻ *Substitute lemon zest and lemon oil for the orange zest and orange oil.*

> **Similar to marshmallow, nougat, pronounced *NEW-gut*, is an aerated candy made from whipped egg whites and sugar syrup. Unlike marshmallow, however, nougat is commonly pressed with weights during the drying process, which makes it dense and chewy rather than light and fluffy.**

INDEX

Almond Bars, 75
Almond Biscotti, 45
Almond Cookies, 69
Almond Pine Nut Macaroons, 100
avoiding contamination, 14
Basic Baking Mix, 13
Brazilian Sugar Cookies, 56
Buttercream Icing, 24
Candied Cherry Walnut Thumbprint Cookies, 42
Caramel Pecan Bars, 80
Cashew Macaroons, 102
Chocolate Chip Cookies, 64
Chocolate Peppermint Biscotti, 46
Chocolate Peppermint Brownies, 90
Chocolate Walnut Fudge, 111
Chocolate-Dipped Florentines, 68
Christmas Sugar Cookies, 28
Classic Chocolate Truffles, 121
Cocoa Chocolate Chip Meringues, 103
Coconut Macaroons, 101
Confectioners' Sugar Glaze, 22
Cornmeal Dried Fruit Cookies, 59
Cranberry Nut Bars, 76
Crispy Peanut Butter Balls, 123
Double Chocolate French Macarons, 99
Dried Fruit Coconut Balls, 124
Dried Fruit Nougat, 126
Egg Paint, 24
egg whites, 94
Fancy French Macarons, 96

Fudgy Hazelnut Brownies, 89
Ginger Shortbread Fingers, 38
Gingerbread People, 31
gluten-free flours and starches, 10
Graham Crackers, 50
Hazelnut Nougat, 117
Holiday Biscotti, 49
Layered Chip and Coconut Bars, 84
Lemon Cookie Ornaments, 36
Lemon Squares, 83
Linzer Cookies, 35
Marble Fudge Brownies, 86
Mexican Chocolate Cookies, 67
Oatmeal Pumpkin Nut Bars, 79
Peanut Butter and Chocolate Layered Brownies, 91
Peanut Butter Chocolate Thumbprint Cookies, 41
Peanut Butter Cookies, 60
Peanut Penuche, 114
Peppermint Pinwheels, 37
Piña Colada Oatmeal Cookies, 63
Praline Meringues, 104
Royal Icing, 23
Snowball Cookies, 55
Southern Pecan Pralines, 112
Spiced Buttery Peanut Brittle, 118
Spritz, 32
sugar stages, 108
Triple Chocolate Hazelnut Cookies, 70
White Chocolate Almond Truffles, 122
White Chocolate Walnut Blondies, 85

About Cider Mill Press Book Publishers

Good ideas ripen with time. From seed to harvest, Cider Mill Press
brings fine reading, information, and entertainment together between
the covers of its creatively crafted books. Our Cider Mill bears fruit
twice a year, publishing a new crop of titles each spring and fall.

Visit us on the Web at
www.cidermillpress.com
or write to us at
12 Port Farm Road
Kennebunkport, Maine 04046